Sunday School Teacher's Syllabus

GARY R. JACKSON

Faithful Life Publishers
North Fort Myers, FL 33903

FaithfulLifePublishers.com

Sunday School Teacher's Syllabus

© 2016 by Gary R. Jackson
ISBN: 978-1-63073-109-0

Published and printed by:
Faithful Life Publishers • North Fort Myers, FL 33903
888.720.0950 • info@FaithfulLifePublishers.com
www.FaithfulLifePublishers.com

All rights reserved. No part of this publication may be reproduced, stored in a retrieval system, or transmitted in any form or by any means—electronic, mechanical, photocopy, recording, or any other—except for brief quotations in printed review, without the prior permission of the author and/or publisher.

Printed in the United States of America

20 19 18 17 16   1 2 3 4 5

TABLE OF CONTENTS

Introduction		e
One:	How To Use This Syllabus	1
Two:	How Do You Become a Sunday School Teacher?	5
Three:	How Do You Know If You Have the Gift of Teaching?	15
Four:	How To Teach	25
Five:	How To Prepare A Lesson	45
Six:	How To Present Your Lesson	63
Seven:	How To Use Different Teaching Methods and Aids	77
Eight:	How To Relate To Your Students	99
Nine:	How To Schedule Your Time	137
Ten:	Discipline - How To Keep Control of Your Class	145
Eleven:	How To Build Your Class	159
Twelve:	How To Lead A Person To Christ	169
Thirteen:	How To Evaluate Your Teaching	179
Final Review		187
Bibliography		195
Answer Key for Learning Exercises		197
Answer Key for Chapter Review (For *Certificate of Completion*)		227
About the Author		235
Exploring the Doctrines Series by the author		236

Certificate of Completion

Earn a ***Certificate of Completion*** by contacting:

Liberty Baptist Church
4249 Bahia Vista Street
Sarasota, FL 34232
(941) 371-8239
www.lbcsarasota.com

INTRODUCTION

After I graduated from high school my father helped me get a job working in a gas station. I didn't know anything about working on cars, so my father thought it would be a good learning experience for me. The manager of the service station told me he would teach me everything I needed to know to work on cars. He gave me one lesson in auto mechanics. He insisted experience is the best teacher. One day he brought this huge a-frame painted sign to the station. He placed it out on the corner where everyone passing through the intersection could see it. The sign, in big letters, said *"Mechanic On Duty 24 Hours."* It gave me heart failure when I read it, for there were times when I ran the station all by myself. The station manager told me not to worry, if somebody came in while he was out. He said, *"Just write up the order and then give me a call, I will tell you what to do."*

After that I went to work every day with fear and trembling, fearful that someone would come in and want a brake job, tune-up, or their transmission repaired. Then one day my greatest fears were realized. A man came in and wanted a tune-up. I did everything I could to convince the man to take his car to the station across the street. But he was determined on having it done at my station. I stalled as long as I could, and finally I pulled the car into the garage and wrote up the order. I remembered what the station manager said, *"Just call me and I will tell you what to do."* Hallelujah! I would just call him and he would tell me what to do. I called and called but there was no answer. That left me with no alternative but to attempt to tune this poor customer's car. I took all the old parts out and put all new ones in. Then I prayed that the car would start. Praise the Lord, it started, but it sounded like an old washing machine. While I was trying to figure out how to tell this fellow that I had never tuned a car before, one of the most blessed sights that I had ever seen appeared. It was my manager driving into the station. The manager finished the job and told me this was the way to learn, by trial and error.

What does this have to do with Sunday School? How many inadequately equipped Sunday School teachers face similar frustration? Many teachers are given one lesson in how to teach a class and then are sent in to do the job. We tell them, *"Experience is the best way to learn to teach. You will learn to be a better teacher by trial and error."* Even though this is what I was always told, I thought there must be a better way.

For years I have searched for a teacher training course that could be used to help train our teachers so they wouldn't have to learn everything by trial and error. Most of the courses that are out on the market deal with philosophy and history of teaching. They do not deal with the practical aspects. There are other programs which are written, I think, with the graduate teaching student in mind. What the Sunday School teachers at my church needed is something simple and practical, that would tell them how to do it.

Another problem I faced throughout the Sunday School year was having teachers leave and new teachers stepping into the class. Every teacher training course I have seen has to be conducted by an instructor. That would mean every time we got a new teacher in our Sunday School it would be necessary to have another training session just for that new teacher. This teacher training course is a self-instructional syllabus that may be used at any time during the year.

This syllabus is designed to train the new teacher or help those who have been teaching for years to do a better job.

CHAPTER ONE
HOW TO USE THIS SYLLABUS

I. Introduction

In elementary school, one day, my teacher announced that we were going to have a math test. She asked us to clear our desks and take out a pencil. Before she handed out the tests, she gave specific instructions to read through the entire test before beginning. Then for emphasis, she repeated the instructions. However, when she began handing out the tests, most of the students immediately began working as fast as they could without so much as looking at the instructions. It wasn't long before several of the students had their hands in the air asking for help from the teacher. They complained that we had never done the kind of problems on the test before. The teacher repeated her instructions to just read the directions. She said, *"If you will do that, you will have no problem with the test."* This did not end the complaining. So the teacher continued repeating the instructions. Finally, the teacher said, *"Your time is up."* There was a moan throughout the class. Then the teacher said, *"Now I want you to look at the very last set of instructions on this test and read them with me."* This is what the instructions said: This is not a test in math, it is a test to see how well you follow instructions. You do not have to work any of the above problems. After you have read this, turn your paper over and wait for further instructions.

I said all of that to say this, if you will read and follow the instructions throughout this syllabus, you should have no problem completing it.

II. What Is A Syllabus?

This syllabus is a complete teacher training course. It is designed so that an individual, desiring to become a Sunday School teacher or improve their teaching, can complete the work on their own. In other words, it is an independent self-study program. However, if the teacher-trainer desires to lecture on the training material, it is very adaptable.

The material was written as a self-study course so a Sunday School teacher could be trained at any time during the year. The teacher-trainees can work at their own pace to complete the course. When the trainee has finished all the work in the syllabus and scored satisfactorily on the final review, the teacher-training certificate in the back of the syllabus may be filled out and signed by an approved teacher-trainer.

III. A Sample of the Syllabus

The Average Sunday School Teacher

I grew up going to Sunday School every Sunday. I had many different teachers. I can remember little things about each of them. I remember one teacher who had a wooden leg. I was afraid of him. Another teacher gave the best object lessons. All week long I looked forward to what he would have for the next Sunday. Then there was a teacher who was always late. He would stand up in front of our class and read the lesson from the Sunday School quarterly. That class was so boring that I didn't want to go to Sunday School. In fact, my father had to spank me on the church steps to get me to go one Sunday.

The average teacher in our Sunday Schools in America is like the last teacher I mentioned in my illustration. The average Sunday School teacher is one of the main reasons many Sunday Schools are not growing today.

Notice a description of the average Sunday School given by Leavitt in, *Teach with Success*. The average teacher is a woman, four out of five are. She is about forty-five years old, the mother of two children. She has a high school education plus one year of college. She has had no teaching experience except that which she received in her own Sunday School. She spends less than an hour a week in preparing her lesson for Sunday, and that usually on Saturday night. In her preparation she relies entirely upon the Bible and quarterly. She usually arrives late and is absent ten Sundays per year. She makes little use of new methods or visuals, she teaches the same way week after week. The average teacher's worst weakness is her self-satisfaction. She feels that she is doing an acceptable job.

LEARNING EXERCISE #1

INSTRUCTIONS: Fill in the blanks from the section you have just read.

1. The _____ _____ _____ teacher is one of the main reasons many Sunday Schools are not growing today.

2. The average Sunday School teacher is a _____ , four out of five are.

3. She is about forty-five years old, the mother of _____ children.

4. She has a high school education plus _____ year of college.

5. She has had no _____ experience except that which she received in her own Sunday School.

6. She spends less than an _____ a _____ in preparing her lesson for Sunday and that usually on Saturday night.

7. In her preparation she relies entirely upon her _____ and _____ .

8. She usually _____ _____ and is absent ten Sundays per year.

9. She makes little use of new methods or visuals, she teaches ____ ____ ____ week after week.

10. The average teacher's worst weakness is her _____ - _____ .

CHAPTER REVIEW (For *Certificate of Completion*)

INSTRUCTIONS: Write "T" if the sentence is true, "F" if the sentence is false.

1. _____ The average Sunday School teacher's worst weakness is her self-satisfaction.
2. _____ The average Sunday School teacher has had lots of teaching experience.
3. _____ The average teacher is a man.
4. _____ The average Sunday School teacher is one of the main reasons many Sunday Schools are not growing today.
5. _____ The average Sunday School teacher has a high school education with one year of college.
6. _____ The average Sunday School teacher spends more than an hour a week in preparing her lesson.
7. _____ The average Sunday School teacher usually prepares her lesson on Saturday night.
8. _____ The average Sunday School teacher in her preparation relies entirely upon her Bible and quarterly.
9. _____ The average Sunday School teacher usually arrives late.
10. _____ The average Sunday School teacher makes little use of new methods or visuals, she teaches the same way week after week.

CHAPTER TWO
HOW DO YOU BECOME A SUNDAY SCHOOL TEACHER?

I. Introduction

One day when I was visiting door to door through my neighborhood, I met a lady at the end of my street who almost snapped my head off when I told her I was an Independent Baptist. She said she would never go to another Independent Baptist Church again. I asked her what happened and she told me that she had attended an Independent Church here in our town and had a terrible experience. She said one day she went to the pastor and told him that she wanted to teach a Sunday School class. Then suddenly this lady flew into a rage and shouted, *"That preacher told me I couldn't teach a class."* I asked, "Did he tell you why?"

"Yes," she replied, *"he told me I would have to get baptized and join the church."* She continued. *"I left that church and I'll never go to another Independent Baptist Church again!"* The preacher was wise not to let that lady teach. After talking with her further, I found that she wasn't even sure of her salvation, but she wanted to teach a Sunday School class!

II. To Be A Sunday School Teacher You Must Be A Saved and Baptized Church Member.

A lot of people say that they are saved or they're Christians. Just what is a Christian? A Christian is a follower of Christ. And in order to be a follower of Christ in deed and in truth, one must, as a sinner, have met Christ, accepted the atonement made by Him for sin, and passed from death unto life. The natural (unsaved) man, being dead in trespasses and sin, cannot follow Christ as a Christian; though he may follow Him as an example. Christ is the Savior of men, and one who follows Christ as a Christian is one who has been saved. It is one thing to be called a Christian and quite another thing to be a Christian. By way of summary, it may be said that a Christian is a human being who has met and accepted Christ alone for the gift of eternal life. As a consequence of this experience of grace, he has become a follower of Christ.

Education, to be Christian, must be conducted by persons who have been redeemed through faith in Jesus Christ, and who thus have a personal relationship to Him. Without the living reality of this experience of salvation through God's grace, a teacher is not a Christian, and teaching can in no sense be called Christian teaching. This is true for several reasons:

- A. First, the aim of Christian education necessitates born again teachers. The transformation of lives, the growth of Christian personalities, the nurturing of pupils toward conformity to the will of God, demand that the teacher be one who possesses high spiritual objectives.

- B. Second, the nature of Christian teaching demands regenerated instructors. Christian teaching is a divine calling, not simply a secular vocation. It is a ministry divinely ordained of God for the purpose of using divinely appointed persons to communicate truths of a divinely inspired book, in order to help pupils lead divine lives. Since the entire process is a divine one, only those who are divinely regenerated by God's Spirit qualify to engage in this ministry. An unsaved person, though religious, does not know God and therefore is incapable of communicating the truth and will of God to others.

- C. Third, the influence of teachers' lives demands that teachers know Christ in salvation. The life, words, actions, attitudes, convictions, and objectives of the teacher who does not know Christ as Savior is unable to influence his pupils with the realities of his own Christian life, because he has none. God's plan is to teach through regenerated personalities whom He indwells.

- D. The spiritual ministry of teaching God's truth has been given to the local church. According to Matthew 28:19, only a person who has been properly baptized and is a member of the local church he wishes to teach in can scripturally carry out the Lord's commission, *"teaching them to observe all things whatsoever I have commanded you."*

LEARNING EXERCISE #1

INSTRUCTIONS: Fill in the blanks from the section you have just read.

1. To be a Sunday School teacher you must be a _____ and _____ church member.

2. A lot of people _____ they are saved or are Christians.

3. A Christian is a _____ of Christ.

4. The natural (unsaved) human, being dead in trespasses and sin, cannot follow Christ as a Christian though he may follow Him as an _____ .

5. Christ is the Savior of men, and one who follows Christ as a Christian is one who has been _____ .

6. It is one thing to be _____ a Christian and quite another thing to be a _____ .

7. Education, to be Christian, must be conducted by persons who have been redeemed through ____ ___ _____ _____ and who thus have a personal relationship to Him.

8. Without the living reality of this experience of salvation through God's grace, a teacher is not a _____, and teaching can in no sense be called _____ teaching.

9. The _____ of Christian education necessitates born again teachers.

10. The _____ of Christian teaching demands regenerated instructors.

11. An unsaved person, though religious, does not know God and therefore is _____ of communicating the _____ and will of God to others.

12. The _____ of teachers lives demands that teachers know Christ in salvation.

13. The spiritual ministry of teaching God's truth has been given to the _____ _____ according to Matthew 28:19.

14. Only a person who has been properly _____ and is a _____ of the local church he wishes to teach in can scripturally carry out the Lord's commission.

15. Are you saved, baptized and a member of the church you wish to teach in? (circle one)   YES   NO   (If your answer is NO then you need to get this taken care of)

III. To Be A Sunday School Teacher You Must Meet the Guidelines Set By Scriptures.

Realizing the importance, privilege and responsibility of serving the Lord Jesus Christ, a Sunday School teacher must adhere to the following guidelines:

A. The Sunday School teacher must have accepted Jesus Christ as their personal Lord and Savior (John 1:12).

B. The Sunday School teacher must have been baptized by immersion as a believer in Jesus Christ, and be a faithful member in all services and activities of the church (Acts 2:41 42; Hebrews 10:25).

C. The Sunday School teacher must believe in the Bible as the inspired word of God and in the literal interpretation of its fundamental truths (II Timothy 3:16 17).

D. The Sunday School teacher must be a doer of the Word and not just a hearer (James 1:22).

E. The Sunday School teacher must practice the Bible method of tithes and offerings through their local church, and will teach their class to do likewise (Genesis 28:22; Malachi 3:8-11).

F. The Sunday School teacher will live their daily lives by precept and example, to be free from all questionable habits and indulgences, such as the use of intoxicating liquors, use of tobacco in any form, and attending any form of worldliness which might prove a stumbling block to others. They try to live daily so that others may see Christ in them (I Corinthians 6:19 20; Romans 14:13; I Thessalonians 5:22).

G. The Sunday School teacher will have a faithful prayer life and pray daily for every member of their class (Ephesians 6:18; I Thessalonians 5:17).

H. The Sunday School teacher will study their Bible faithfully in order that they might increase their knowledge of the Word (II Timothy 2:15).

I. The Sunday School teacher will adequately prepare their Sunday School lesson and teach from an open Bible (Ezra 7:10).

J. The Sunday School teacher will regularly attend the scheduled teachers' meetings (Luke 16:12).

K. The Sunday School teacher will visit prospects and visitors and is also responsible for the absentees in their class, calling upon them in person, if at all possible, or getting in touch with them in some other way to learn the reason for their absence (Ephesians 6:7; Acts 20:20).

L. The Sunday School teacher will notify the Sunday School Superintendent as soon as they know that they will not be able to teach (I Corinthians 4:12).

M. The Sunday School teacher will be a soul winner, their highest aim as a teacher will be to help their class members know Christ and one day accept Him as their personal Savior (Proverbs 11:30).

N. The Sunday School teacher will have an attitude of love (I Corinthians 13:1 3).

O. The Sunday School teacher will be on time (Romans 12:11).

P. The Sunday School teacher will lean upon the Lord as their strength, and the Holy Spirit as their guide in the accomplishing of these Scriptural standards (Philippians 4:13).

Q. The Sunday School teacher will have the gift of teaching (Ephesians 4:11).

After reading these guidelines for teachers some may not want to be, or even think that they are qualified to be, a Sunday School teacher. But if a person has the gift of teaching they must use it or else they will lose it. In the next chapter, The Gift of Teaching, will be dealt with thoroughly.

LEARNING EXERCISE #2

INSTRUCTIONS: Fill in the blanks from the section you have just read.

1. To be a Sunday School teacher you must meet the guidelines set by _____ .

2. The Sunday School teacher must have accepted _____ as their personal Lord and Savior.

3. The Sunday School teacher must have been baptized by _____ as a believer in Jesus Christ.

4. The Sunday School teacher must believe in the Bible as the _____ .

5. The Sunday School teacher must be a _____ of the Word and not just a _____ .

6. The Sunday School teacher will practice the Bible method of _____ and _____ through their local church.

7. What are two examples of questionable habits that a teacher should abstain from?
   a. _____
   b. _____

8. The Sunday School teacher should try to live daily so that others may see _____ in them.

9. The Sunday School teacher will pray daily for every member of their _____ .

10. The Sunday School teacher will _____ their Bible faithfully.

11. List the three groups the Sunday School teacher must visit:
    a. _____
    b. _____
    c. _____

12. The Sunday School teacher will notify the Sunday School _____ as soon as they know that they will not be able to teach.

13. The Sunday School teacher will be a soul winner, their highest aim as a teacher will be to help their class members _____ and one day accept Him as their personal Savior.

14. The Sunday School teacher will have an attitude of _____ .

15. The Sunday School teacher will be on _____ .

16. The Sunday School teacher will _____ upon the Lord as their strength, and the Holy Spirit as their _____ .

17. The Sunday School teacher will have the _____ _____ _____ .

CHAPTER REVIEW (For *Certificate of Completion*)

INSTRUCTIONS: Write "T" if the sentence is true, "F" if the sentence is false.

1. _____ To be a Sunday School teacher you don't have to be a church member.

2. _____ A lot of people say they are saved or a Christian.

3. _____ An unsaved person is a follower of Christ.

4. _____ Christ is the Savior and one who follows Christ as a Christian is one who has been saved.

5. _____ There is no difference in being called a Christian and being a Christian.

6. _____ The aim and nature of Christian education necessitates born again teachers.

7. _____ An unsaved person, though religious does not know God and therefore is incapable of communicating the truth and will of God to others.

8. _____ The spiritual ministry of teaching God's truth has been given to the local church according to Matthew 1:1.

9. _____ Only a person who has been properly baptized and is a member of the local church he wishes to teach in can Scripturally carry out the Lord's commission.

10. _____ To be a Sunday School teacher you must meet the guidelines set by Scriptures.

11. _____ The Sunday School teacher must have been sprinkled as a baby.

12. _____ The Sunday School teacher must believe in the Bible as the inspired Word of God.

13. _____ The Sunday School teacher must be a doer of the Word and not just a hearer.

14. _____ The Sunday School teacher will practice the Bible method of tithes and offerings only if they can afford to.

15. _____ Two examples of questionable habits that a teacher should abstain from are working on the Sabbath and eating meat.

16. _____ The Sunday School teacher should try to live daily so that others may see Christ in them.

17. _____ The Sunday School teacher will pray and read their Bible daily.

18. _____ The Sunday School teacher will visit: prospects, visitors, absentees, and class members.

19. _____ The Sunday School teacher will be a soul winner.

20. _____ The Sunday School teacher can be late once in a while.

CHAPTER THREE
HOW DO YOU KNOW IF YOU HAVE THE GIFT OF TEACHING?

I. Introduction

A young man came to me and told me he thought he had the gift of teaching. He said he believed God was going to use him to do something great. At that time we needed someone to teach the teen class. He said he believed he could do a great job with the teens. The second week that he taught the class in the middle of the Sunday School hour this young man walked out of his class of teenagers and left the church. I thought maybe he got sick or something. He called me later that day and told me that the reason he walked out is because they wouldn't listen to him. He told me he believed he would do better with the young adult class. So I arranged for him to take that class. There were fifteen to twenty people when he took the class. After about a month it had dwindled to five.

I discovered the hard way that some folks don't have the gift of teaching.

II. What Is the Gift of Teaching?

There is much confusion and ignorance regarding the spiritual gifts. Most of the books used to do the research for this syllabus ignored the subject altogether. Only one book examined the subject thoroughly, Roy Zuck's book, *Spiritual Power in Your Teaching*, and it provides the basis of this chapter. Several authors indicated that they believed that every Christian was to be a teacher. In many instances the spiritual gifts are not even considered when searching for Sunday School teachers. I read about a substitute who was asked to fill in for one Sunday. After seventeen years of teaching, she wonders if this is going to become a permanent job. Another teacher recounted that her teaching career began because she arrived late for church one Sunday morning. She was the only person in the hallway when the Sunday School Superintendent realized he was short one teacher. He spotted her, and a teacher was born!

Before we can properly understand the specific gift of teaching we must consider the "Gifts" in general.

- A. First, it is clear from the Scripture that every believer has some gift (I Corinthians 12:7, 11; Romans 12:3; I Peter 4:10; Ephesians 4:7). The gifts were given so that every believer has a function in the local church (Romans 12:5; I Corinthians 12:27; Ephesians 4:8, 12).

- B. Second, there is a diversity of gifts, yet unity, among them. The lists of gifts are given in (Romans 12:68; I Corinthians 12:4-11, 28-30; and Ephesians 4:7-12). There are at least sixteen spiritual gifts enumerated in the New Testament; but, there is only one Spirit who gives the gifts with one aim in mind, to minister to the unity of the Body, (Ephesians 4:13, 16). Just as there are many parts to one physical body, so there are many members with varied gifts in the one body of Christ (I Corinthians 12:18-20; Ephesians 4:4).

- C. Third, spiritual gifts are of divine origin and sovereignly bestowed by God. Each member is placed in the body with a particular gift or gifts, according to God's sovereign will. God divides *"to each one severally as He will"* (I Corinthians 12:11). An attitude of humility should accompany the exercise of spiritual gifts, for they are all undeserved.

- D. Fourth, some gifts are permanent, while others were temporary, having been exercised only in the apostolic period. The gifts possessed by some believers in the church today are teaching, evangelism, pastoring, exhorting, giving, showing mercy, helping, administering, discerning spirits, and faith. Among the temporary gifts are apostleship, prophecy, performing miracles, healing, tongues, and interpreting tongues.

- E. Fifth, spiritual gifts are given for a twofold goal: the edifying of the body of Christ, and ascribing glory to the Lord (I Peter 4:11;Ephesians 4:12).

- F. Now that we have noted the general gifts, look at the specific gift of teaching.

1. The gift of teaching is of primary importance in the ministry of Christian education in the local church. It is one of the major gifts, for it is mentioned specifically in each of the three lists of gifts in the New Testament (Romans 12:7-8; I Corinthians 12:28; Ephesians 4:11).

2. The gift of teaching is also closely associated with preaching (Acts 5:42; I Timothy 2:7; II Timothy 1:11), and is closely linked with the gift of pastoring. One way in which a pastor or shepherd cared for his flock is by teaching them. The pastor-teacher compares to the "teaching priest" of the Old Testament (II Chronicles 15:3).

3. The teaching gift is of primary importance in the edifying of the church. Since the gifts are given for ministering to the body of Christ, it is clear that those who are most effective in this spiritual task of edification are those who possess and are cultivating the gift of teaching. Many seek to be teachers but are not met with any degree of spiritual success in their efforts because they are without the teaching gift.

4. The teaching gift, like other spiritual gifts, is a supernatural ability. The gift of teaching is a supernatural, Spirit endowed ability to expound (explain and apply) the truth of God. Spiritual gifts clearly pertain to the spiritual birth of a believer rather than to his natural birth. This is clear for several reasons:

    a. Obviously, the Scriptures never speak of non-Christians possessing spiritual gifts.

    b. Spiritual gifts are more than manifestations of human ability because they are called "gifts."

    c. They are given for edifying the body of Christ, and therefore are related to the believer's new nature.

    d. Spiritual gifts are called manifestations of the Spirit (I Corinthians 12:7).

Sometimes after a person gets saved he or she receives spiritual gifts which are in accord with pre-conversion natural abilities. The spiritual gifts do three things to those natural abilities: they enhance them, channel them into spiritual spheres of ministry, and quicken them to accomplish the task.

LEARNING EXERCISE #1

INSTRUCTIONS: Fill in the blanks from the section you have just read.

1. There is much confusion and ignorance regarding the _____ _____.

2. In many instances the spiritual gifts are not even considered when searching for Sunday School _____.

3. Before we can properly understand the specific gift of teaching we must consider the gifts in _____.

4. It is clear from the Scripture that every believer has some _____.

5. There is a _____ of gifts, yet _____ among them.

6. There are at least _____ spiritual gifts enumerated in the New Testament.

7. Spiritual gifts are of _____ origin and _____ bestowed by God.

8. God divides "to _____ _____ *severally as He will*" (I Corinthians 12:11).

9. Some gifts are _____, while others were _____ having been experienced only in the apostolic period.

10. List three permanent gifts and three temporary gifts:

   Permanent: Temporary:

   1. _____   1. _____

   2. _____   2. _____

   3. _____   3. _____

11. Spiritual gifts are given for two reasons, name them:

   1. _____

   2. _____

12. The gift of teaching is of primary importance in the ministry of _____ _____ in the local church.

13. The gift of teaching is also closely associated with _____.

14. The teaching gift is of primary importance in the _____ of the church.

15. Many seek to be teachers but are not met with any degree of spiritual success in their efforts because they are without the _____.

16. The teaching gift, like other spiritual gifts, is a _____.

17. The gift of teaching is a supernatural, spirit endowed ability to _____ (explain and apply) the truth of God.

18. Spiritual gifts clearly pertain to the spiritual birth of a believer rather than to his _____.

19. Scriptures never speak of non-Christians possessing _____.

20. List the three things the spiritual gifts do to natural abilities.

   1. _____

   2. _____

   3. _____

III. How Do You Know If You Have the Gift of Teaching?

It is the duty of each believer, in reference to spiritual gifts, to discover what his gift is and then to develop and exercise it to the glory of God. Each believer must discover whether or not God has given them the gift of teaching. It is one thing to have the gift of teaching, but it is another to have the gift of teaching and know it. It is conceivable that some believers possess the gift of teaching but are totally unaware of the fact. Having never exercised the gift, they may not be aware of this latent spiritually endowed ability. Either they have not been instructed about the matter of spiritual gifts, or they are out of fellowship with the Lord and are thus incapable of receiving and appropriating spiritual truth.

How, then, may believers determine if they have the gift of teaching? Several guideposts may be mentioned:

A. As mentioned in the previous section, sometimes the gift is given in accord with the natural ability of teaching. Therefore, if a person were gifted as a teacher before he was saved, he should consider whether this may be his spiritual gift for edifying the church. It may or may not be.

B. Another means of determining whether one has the gift of teaching is to minister in several capacities in the local church and elsewhere. If one possesses the gift of teaching, either he or others or both may discover his latent ability, as he ministers in a teaching capacity.

C. Another way by which this gift may be determined is the evident blessing of God in one's teaching. Often spiritual results and blessings evidenced in one's ministry are a divine token that the believer has struck on that which God has intended as his prescribed ministry to the body of Christ. All this applies to laymen as well as to Christians in "full-time" Christian teaching capacities. Obviously, a Christian cannot accurately ascertain God's intentions for him in this direction unless he is in the center of God's will, filled by the Spirit.

To discover a spiritual gift is only the first step toward its effective utilization. As a believer lives in God's will, they are then in the proper spiritual condition for developing his gift of teaching. The exhortation to develop and increase the effectiveness of one's gift is stated at least three times in the Bible. Twice Paul addressed Timothy regarding his spiritual gift (I Timothy 4:14-15; II Timothy 1:6). Paul told him first not to "neglect" it, then he told him to "stir up" the gift that God gave to him.

The exercising of spiritual gifts is to be done as an act of stewardship. I Peter 4:10 says, "As every man hath received the gift, even so minister the same one to another, as good stewards of the manifold grace of God." A spiritual gift is an entrustment, as well as an enablement and endowment. If a Christian has the teaching gift, he is responsible to care for it as a steward would his master's household.

Various means by which we may develop the gift of teaching are: Observing others who have the gift, getting training and schooling in how to teach, and gaining teaching experience. As a good steward of that which God has sovereignly bestowed, Christian teachers will be anxious to do all they can to improve and make the best use of his gift.

LEARNING EXERCISE #2

INSTRUCTIONS: Fill in the blanks from the section you have just read.

1. List the three duties of every believer in reference to their spiritual gifts:

    1. _____

    2. _____

    3. _____

2. Each believer must discover whether or not God has given him the _____.

3. It is conceivable that some believers possess the gift of teaching but are totally _____ of the fact.

4. List two reasons why a person may not be aware of the gift of teaching:

    1. _____

    2. _____

5. If a person were gifted as a teacher _____ he was saved, he should _____ whether this may be his spiritual gift for edifying the church.

6. Another means of determining whether one has the gift of teaching is to minister in _____ in the local church.

7. Another token by which this gift may be determined is the evident blessing of God on one's teaching, often _____ and _____ evidence in one's ministry are a divine token that the believer has struck on that which God has intended as his prescribed ministry to the body of Christ.

8. Christians cannot accurately ascertain God's intentions for them in this direction unless they are in the _____ of God's _____ , filled by the Spirit.

9. To discover a spiritual gift is only the _____ toward its effective utilization.

10. The exhortation to develop and increase the effectiveness of ones gift is stated at least _____ times in the Bible.

11. The exercising of spiritual gifts is to be done as an act of _____.

12. A spiritual gift is an _____, as well as an _____ and _____.

13. If Christians have the teaching gift, they are _____ to care for it as a steward would their master's household.

14. List the three means by which one may develop his gift of teaching:

    1. _____
    2. _____
    3. _____

15. A Christian teacher will be _____ to do all he can to _____ and make the best use this gift.

CHAPTER REVIEW (For *Certificate of Completion*)

INSTRUCTIONS: Write a "T" if the sentence is true, or an "F" if the sentence is false.

1. _____ There is much confusion and ignorance regarding the spiritual gifts.

2. _____ It is clear from the Scripture that every believer has some gift.

3. _____ There are at least sixteen spiritual gifts innumerated in the New Testament.

4. _____ The gifts of teaching, tongues and giving are permanent gifts.

5. _____ The gifts of apostleship, healing and prophecy are temporary gifts.

6. _____ Spiritual gifts are given for edifying the body of Christ and ascribing glory to the Lord.

7. _____ The gift of teaching is of primary importance in the ministry of Christian education.

8. _____ The teaching gift, like other spiritual gifts, is a natural ability.

9. _____ The gift of teaching is a supernatural, Spirit-endowed ability to expound (explain and apply) the truth of God.

10. _____ Spiritual gifts clearly pertain to the spiritual birth of a believer rather than to his natural birth.

11. _____ Scriptures speak of non-Christians possessing spiritual gifts.

12. _____ There are three things the spiritual gifts do to natural abilities: enhance, channel, and quicken.

13. _____ Every believer has three duties in reference to their spiritual gifts: discover, to develop and to exercise.

14. _____ Each believer must discover whether or not God has given them a gift.

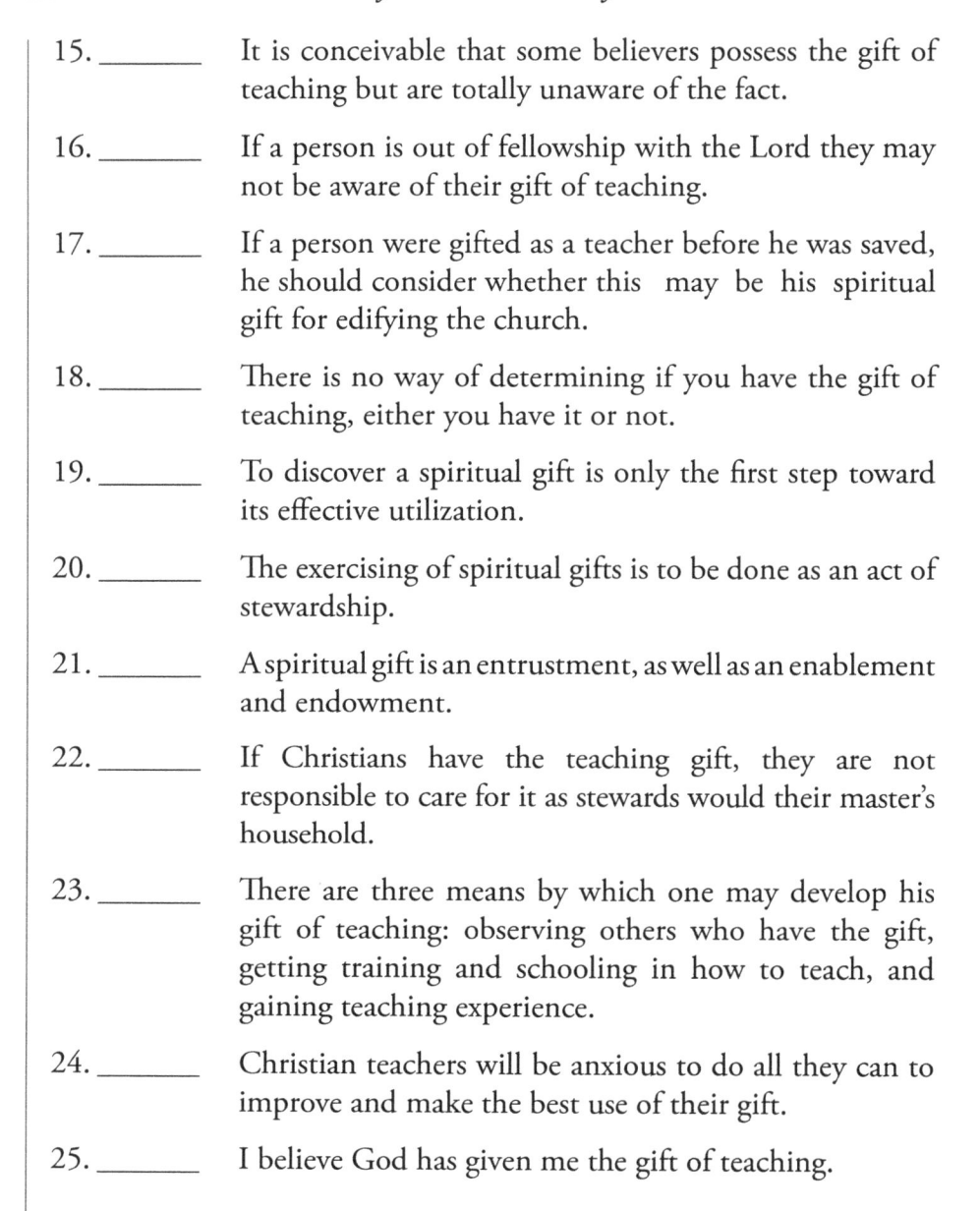

15. _____ It is conceivable that some believers possess the gift of teaching but are totally unaware of the fact.

16. _____ If a person is out of fellowship with the Lord they may not be aware of their gift of teaching.

17. _____ If a person were gifted as a teacher before he was saved, he should consider whether this may be his spiritual gift for edifying the church.

18. _____ There is no way of determining if you have the gift of teaching, either you have it or not.

19. _____ To discover a spiritual gift is only the first step toward its effective utilization.

20. _____ The exercising of spiritual gifts is to be done as an act of stewardship.

21. _____ A spiritual gift is an entrustment, as well as an enablement and endowment.

22. _____ If Christians have the teaching gift, they are not responsible to care for it as stewards would their master's household.

23. _____ There are three means by which one may develop his gift of teaching: observing others who have the gift, getting training and schooling in how to teach, and gaining teaching experience.

24. _____ Christian teachers will be anxious to do all they can to improve and make the best use of their gift.

25. _____ I believe God has given me the gift of teaching.

CHAPTER FOUR
HOW TO TEACH

I. Introduction

Several years ago after a Wednesday night Bible study I gave a quiz over the sermon to see if the people learned anything. I had one side of the congregation in competition against the other side. The people seemed to enjoy it, especially the kids. I continued this all summer, then all fall. I discovered that the people were really learning. The thing that amazed me was the children and teenagers and how much they learned. At times I would be preaching and thinking to myself 'these people are not hearing a word that I am saying.' But, after I finished preaching and gave a quiz, the ones who seemed as though they were asleep or a million miles away would be the first ones with the answers. The people were learning from my teaching.

One day I came out of a store and saw a lady who had moved away from our area with her husband a number of years earlier. She was as surprised to see me as I was to see her. She told me they were attending a convention. In the course of our conversation she told me over and over how much they had learned while they were at our church. She said they didn't realize it until they moved away and attended another church. She said her husband was even elected chairman of the deacons. I could hardly believe my ears. This fellow was one of those who you would think was letting the sermon go in one ear and out the other. But he learned more from my teaching than I thought or even realized until they moved.

Just putting a person in a room full of students and giving the person the title "teacher," does not make one a teacher. A person is not a teacher until students learn.

What facilitates learning? What factors or conditions are necessary for effective learning?

How do pupils best learn? How can teachers cooperate with the Holy Spirit's laws which govern good learning?

Pupils learn best when they are motivated, when the subject matter is relevant to them, when they are actively involved, and when they are ready to learn.

The classic text, *The Seven Laws of Teaching*, by John Milton Gregory, sets the pattern for the work of a teacher by presenting a clear and simple statement of the important factors governing the act of teaching. Gregory's book provides the basis for the laws of teaching as presented in this chapter.

II. The Law of the Teacher

The effective teacher needs to know several things.

- A. First, the teacher must know the Lord personally. To teach others, Christian teachers must be in vital union with Christ, filled with the Word and the Spirit. The single most important factor that influences learning is the life and personality of the teacher. This is because:

    1. Teaching techniques are of little use unless they are used by one through whose life the truth and love of God radiate.

    2. Christian truths are better understood when seen in life.

    3. Lives are impressed and changed more by truths they see demonstrated than by those they merely hear spoken.

- B. Secondly, the effective teacher must know their pupils intimately. A personal interest in and an understanding and appreciation of each pupil's problems and needs contributes to a close personal relationship between teacher and pupil which, in turn, fosters learning. Knowing the backgrounds, interests, difficulties, ambitions, attitudes, needs and levels of maturity of individual pupils enables teachers to select the most appropriate methods and teaching procedures. The more intimately teachers know their pupils, the better equipped they are to meet their needs. As they come to know and work with his pupils as individuals, the Christian teachers can more easily direct them, with the aid of the Holy Spirit, to solutions found in God's Holy Word.

C. Thirdly, the effective teacher must know the lesson thoroughly. They should know more than they have time to teach, not just enough to fill the time. This requires earnest study and investigation in order to have a grasp of the complete lesson. Teachers who master their subject can be at ease as they direct their classes. They are prepared to answer the unexpected questions and problems that are likely to arise in the teaching situation.

LEARNING EXERCISE #1

INSTRUCTIONS: Fill in the blanks from the section you have just read.

1. The teacher must know the Lord _____ .

2. To teach others, Christian teachers must be in vital union with Christ, filled with the _____ and the _____ .

3. The single most important factor that influences learning is the _____ and _____ of the teacher.

4. The single most important factor that influences learning is the life and personality of the teacher, give three reasons for this:
    a. _____
    b. _____
    c. _____

5. Effective teachers must know their pupils _____.

6. A personal interest in and an understanding and appreciation of each pupils problems and needs contribute to a close personal relationship between teachers and pupils which, in turn, fosters _____ .

7. The more intimately teachers know their pupils, the better equipped they are to meet their _____ .

8. The effective teacher must know the lesson _____.

9. They should know more than they have time to teach, not just enough to _____.

10. Teachers who master their subject can be at _____ as they direct their classes.

The Law of the Learner

The learner must attend, with interest, the material to be learned (lesson). First, you must gain and hold their attention. Sustained attention is dependent on interest. It is comparatively easy to gain and hold the attention of an interested student. An imperative command or some clever eye-catching trick may temporarily attract attention, but genuine interest alone will sustain it.

Attention and interest are directly related to motivation. Motivated learning is that which is desired by the student. The quickest route to motivated learning is by gearing the lesson to the needs of the student.

Motivating learning simply means making learning desirable or desired. It is causing pupils to want to learn. It is important that Christian teachers understand this principle so that they can use proper motivational factors and can lead their pupils to want to learn, rather than coercing them to learn.

Motivation facilitates learning. When pupils are motivated to learn, they learn more quickly and the results are more lasting. The stronger the motivation, the more rapid and effective the learning.

A. There are two kinds of motivation: internal and external. Elmer Towns, in his training course, discusses these under the chapter entitled *"The Law of Motivation."* He lists four basic internal motivations.

1. The first internal motivation is "protect me" (self-preservation). What will benefit me? What will save my skin? What will make me a more popular

person? What will make me better liked by others? What will give me more influence?

2. The second internal motivation is "exalt me" (recognition). This may be as small as words of praise. It may be calling people by name, or it may be simply asking everyone who brought a friend to stand. It may be a ribbon, a button, a card that says, *"This student did something important."* While a tangible reward will not move some students, public recognition will cause them to exert amazing effort.

3. The third internal motivation is "accept me" (social acceptance). All students want to belong. Children want to belong to a gang or a clique. Teenage boys want to belong to a girl and visa versa. Businessmen want to be in the power circle. Belonging is a natural motivation for everyone.

4. The last internal motivation is "love me" (affection). Love is one of the deepest needs people have. Students must realize that God loves them. This realization comes first by our teaching it from the Bible. It comes second by offering them His love in salvation. And third, by our love for them. Love is giving yourself to the one you love.

B. There are seven external sources of motivation, according to Elmer Towns:

1. The first external motivation is "bandwagon." The bandwagon principle motivates students because they become involved when other students are involved. This involves pressure of self-acceptance because they want to do as others do and be with them. This principle comes from the phrase, *"climbing on the bandwagon."*

2. The second external motivation is "statistics." Students and teachers alike may be motivated by accurate records of certain statistics within each class. That is

because they see how they measure up to a standard. A record of attendance and participation should be communicated. If a weekly sticker is added to a chart, for example, both teacher and student will know exactly where the student stands in relation to others.

3. The third external motivation is "praise." When the teacher gives honest commendation, one of the students basic needs is being met, therefore, the student is motivated.

4. The fourth external motivation is "rebuke." Some students are motivated by criticism, rebuke, or confrontation for their lack of achievement or effort. However, it must be given firmly and consistently with the teachers earnest desire to communicate God's truth, not with sarcasm or ridicule.

5. The fifth external motivation is "testimony" (either verbal or visual). When a teacher shares how they solved a problem or what a Bible verse means to them, the pupil is motivated to listen and learn.

6. The sixth external motivation is "illustration." Whereas a testimony is a personal story from the life of a teacher, an illustration is from someone else's life.

7. The seventh external motivation is "peer pressure." Peer pressure motivates students. When the majority of students are involved, peer pressure is so great that it motivates the learning process.

LEARNING EXERCISE #2

INSTRUCTIONS: Fill in the blanks from the section you have just read.

1. The learner must attend with interest the material to be _____ .

2. The first thing you must do is gain and hold their _____ .

3. An imperative command or some clever eye-catching trick may temporarily attract attention but _____ _____ alone will sustain it.

4. _____ and _____ are directly related to motivation.

5. Motivating learning simply means making learning _____ or _____ .

6. Motivation facilitates _____ .

7. When pupils are motivated to learn, they learn more quickly and the results are more _____ .

8. What are the two kinds of motivation?

   a. _____

   b. _____

9. List four basic internal motivations:

   a. _____

   b. _____

   c. _____

   d. _____

10. List the seven external sources of motivation:

    a. _____

    b. _____

    c. _____

    d. _____

    e. _____

    f. _____

    g. _____

The Law of Language

Language is the medium of communication between the pupil and teacher. It must be understood by both. It must have the same meaning for both.

Ordinarily, you (the teacher) will have a larger vocabulary than the students. To communicate effectively, however, you must limit yourself to the language of the students. If you fail or refuse to adjust to the students' language, the instruction will not be comprehended. Use language clear and vivid to both you and your students.

The language will differ for every age and department in the church. To observe the law of the language, Gregory suggests that you should do the following:

A. Study constantly and carefully the language of the students.

B. Secure from the students as full a statement as possible of their knowledge of the subject.

C. Express yourself as far as possible in the language of your students.

D. Use the simplest and the fewest words that will express your meaning.

E. Use short sentences, of the simplest construction.

F. To clarify meaning, repeat your thought in another language, if possible, with greater simplicity.

G. Help the meaning of the words by illustrations.

H. When it is necessary to teach a new word, give the idea before the word.

I. Try to increase the number of the students' words, and at the same time to improve the clearness of meaning.

J. Encourage students to talk freely.

K. Test frequently the students' understanding of the words that you use.

Smaller children think literally. For this reason, teachers of children should avoid figurative language, using literal terms that are within the experience of the students.

LEARNING EXERCISE #3

INSTRUCTIONS: Fill in the blanks from the section you have just read.

1. Language is the medium of communication between the pupil and _____ .
2. Language must be _____ by both.
3. Language must have the same _____ for both.
4. Ordinarily, you, the teacher, will have a larger _____ than the students.
5. To communicate effectively you must limit yourself to the _____ .
6. The language will differ for every age and department in the _____ .
7. Study constantly and carefully the language of the _____ .
8. To clarify meaning, repeat your thought in other language, if possible with greater _____ .
9. Help the meaning of the words by _____ .
10. Smaller children think _____ .

V. The Law of the Lesson

The truth to be taught must be learned through truth already known. If the subject is wholly new, then a known point must be sought by showing some likeness of the new to something known and familiar.

Learning must proceed by linking one fact or concept to another. Each idea mastered becomes a part of the knowledge of the pupil and serves as a starting point for a fresh advance. It must be remembered that facts are linked together by association, by resemblances of one sort or another. Each fact leads to, and explains, another. The old reveals the new; the new confirms and corrects the old. Thus, the very nature of knowledge compels us to seek the new through the aid of the old.

New knowledge takes its meaning from what is already known and familiar. A cloud left upon the lesson of yesterday casts its shadow over the lesson of today. On the other hand, the thoroughly mastered lesson throws great light on the succeeding ones.

To observe the law of the lesson, you should be aware of several related procedures:

Find out what your pupils know of the subject you wish to teach them. This is your starting point.

A. Make the most of the pupils' knowledge and experience.

B. Relate every lesson as much as possible to former lessons, and with the pupils' knowledge and experience.

C. Arrange your presentation so that each step of the lesson shall lead easily and naturally to the next.

Find illustrations in the most common and most familiar objects suitable for the purpose.

LEARNING EXERCISE #4

INSTRUCTIONS: Fill in the blanks from the section you have just read.

1. The truth to be taught must be learned through truth already _____ .

2. If the subject is wholly new, then a known point must be sought by showing some likeness of the new to something _____ and _____ .

3. Learning must proceed by linking one fact or _____ to another.

4. Each idea _____ becomes a part of the knowledge of the pupil and serves as a _____ point for a fresh advance.

5. _____ _____ takes its meaning from what is already known and familiar.

6. A _____ left upon the lesson of yesterday casts its _____ over the lesson of today.

7. Find out what your pupils know of the _____ you wish to teach them.

8. Relate every lesson as much as possible to former lessons, and with the pupils _____ and _____ .

9. Arrange your presentation so that each step of the lesson shall lead _____ and _____ to the next.

10. Find illustrations in the most _____ and most _____ objects suitable for the purpose.

VI. The Law of the Teaching Process

The teacher must awaken and set in action the mind of the pupil, arousing his self-activities. True teaching is not that which gives knowledge, but that which stimulates pupils to gain it.

It is not enough for students to learn Bible facts, they must begin to live Bible truths. Your job is not complete until you arouse interest on the part of your students and help them begin to make the Bible teaching a part of their own lives.

To accomplish this, you must deal with students as individuals, leading them to think for themselves. If your students do not learn to think for themselves, there will be little lasting results. The learning processes are quickened when students become independent investigators. Yet teachers are necessary elements in the process as well. Among other things, good teachers provide favorable conditions for self-learning. They do not merely impart knowledge but stimulate their students to acquire it. They motivate their students and set an example of earnest, serious scholarship and make available the resources students need to do independent study. The pupil's education begins as soon as he begins to ask questions.

Notice some important considerations:

A. Adapt lessons and assignments to the ages and attainments of the pupils.

B. Relate to the environment and needs of the pupils.

C. Use questions to excite the learners' interests in the subject.

D. Repress your impatience, which cannot wait for the pupil to explain himself, and which tends to take his words out of his mouth.

E. Repress the desire to tell all you know or think about a lesson or subject.

F. Observe each student to see that his or her mind is not wandering.

G. Give the pupil time to think. Teach the pupil to ask: What? Why? How?

LEARNING EXERCISE #5

INSTRUCTIONS: Fill in the blanks from the section you have just read.

1. The teacher must awaken and set in action the mind of the pupil, arousing his _____ - _____ .

2. True teaching is not that which gives knowledge, but that which _____ pupils to gain it.

3. It is not enough for students to learn _____ _____ .

4. The student must begin to _____ Bible truths.

5. If your students do not learn to _____ for themselves, there will be few lasting results.

6. The learning processes are quickened when students become _____ investigators.

7. Among other things, good teachers provide favorable conditions for _____ - _____ .

8. Teachers motivate their students and set an example of earnest, serious scholarship and make available the resources students need to do _____ _____ .

9. The pupil's education begins as soon as he begins to _____ questions.

10. The teacher should teach the pupil to ask what three questions:

    a. _____

    b. _____

    c. _____

VII. The Law of the Learning Process

The pupil must reproduce in their own mind the truth to be learned. True learning is not memorization and repetition of the words and ideas of the teacher. The pupil must reproduce in their own minds the truth to be learned. The work of education, contrary to common understanding, is much more the work of the pupil than of the teacher. No lesson is fully learned until it is traced to its connections with life. Every fact has its relation to life, and every principle its applications. Until these are known, facts and principles are idle. The learning process is not complete until this stage has been reached.

Nowhere are faults in teaching more frequent or more serious than in the Sunday School. *"Always learning, but never able to come to a knowledge of the truth,"* tells the sad story of many a Sunday School class.

The progressive phases of the learning process are:

A. Knows what the lesson says and can repeat or recite it.

B. Has an understanding of the thought.

C. Can translate the thought accurately into his own or other words without detriment to the meaning.

D. Seeks evidence. Does not only believe what the lesson says, but knows why he believes.

E. Finds a use for what he has learned; applies his knowledge to his practical, everyday life.

LEARNING EXERCISE #6

INSTRUCTIONS: Fill in the blanks from the section you have just read.

1. The pupils must reproduce in their own _____ the truth to be learned.

2. True learning is not _____ and _____ of the words and ideas of the teacher.

3. The pupil must reproduce in their own mind the _____ to be learned.

4. The work of education, contrary to common understanding, is much more the work of the _____ than of the _____ .

5. No lesson is fully _____ until it is traced to its connections with life.

6. Every fact has its relation to life, and every principle its _____ .

7. Nowhere are faults in teaching more frequent or more serious than in the _____ _____ .

8. What is the final phase of the learning process?
    a. _____
    b. _____
    c. _____

VIII. The Law of Review

The completion, test and confirmation of the work of teaching must be made by review and application. A review is more than repetition. A machine may repeat a process, but only an intelligent agent can review it. The repetition done by a machine is a second movement, precisely like the first; a repetition by the mind, is the rethinking of a thought.

A new lesson or a fresh topic never reveals all of itself at first. Even in the best studied book, we are often surprised to find fresh truths and new meanings in passages which we had read, perhaps again and again. Especially this is true of the Bible, in which the latest study is the richest and most interesting.

Frequent repetitions are valuable to correct memorization and aid ready recall. Memory depends upon the association of idea; recalling those ideas which had been linked by some past association. Each review establishes new associations, while at the same time it familiarizes and strengthens the old.

- A. The chief aims of review are:
    1. To perfect knowledge.
    2. To confirm knowledge.
    3. To render this knowledge ready and useful.
- B. The value of review is:
    1. Power of repetition.
    2. Lapse of time changes; point of view.
    3. Survey of lesson from a new standpoint.
    4. Finding of fresh truth and new meanings.
    5. Becomes woven into the very fabric of thought.
- C. The review of lessons should be:
    1. More than mere repetition.
    2. Thorough restudy of the lessons; a careful resurvey.
    3. Interesting, challenging.

LEARNING EXERCISE #7

INSTRUCTIONS: Fill in the blanks from the section you have just read.

1. The completion, test and confirmation of the work of teaching must be made by _____ and _____

2. A review is more than _____ .

3. A machine may repeat a process, but only an _____ agent can review it.

4. A repetition by the mind is the _____ of a thought.

5. A new lesson or a fresh topic never reveals all of _____ at first.

6. Even in the best studied book, we are often surprised to find fresh _____ and new _____ in passages which we had read perhaps again and again.

7. Frequent _____ are valuable to correct memorization and aid ready recall.

8. _____ depends upon the association of ideas; recalling those ideas which had been linked by some past association.

9. Each review establishes new associations, while at the same time it _____ and _____ the old.

10. List the chief aims of review:

    a. _____

    b. _____

    c. _____

11. List the value of review:

   a. _____

   b. _____

   c. _____

   d. _____

   e. _____

12. List what the review of lesson should be:

   a. _____

   b. _____

   c. _____

CHAPTER REVIEW (For *Certificate of Completion*)
INSTRUCTIONS: Write "T" if the sentence is true "F" if the sentence is false.

1. _____ The Sunday School teacher must know the Lord personally.

2. _____ The single most important factor that influences learning is the life and personality of the teacher.

3. _____ The effective teacher doesn't have to know their pupil intimately.

4. _____ The effective teacher doesn't have to know the lesson thoroughly.

5. _____ The teacher should know more than they have time to teach, not just enough to fill the time.

6. _____ The learner must attend with interest the material to be learned.

7. _____ The second thing you must do is gain and hold their genuine interest.

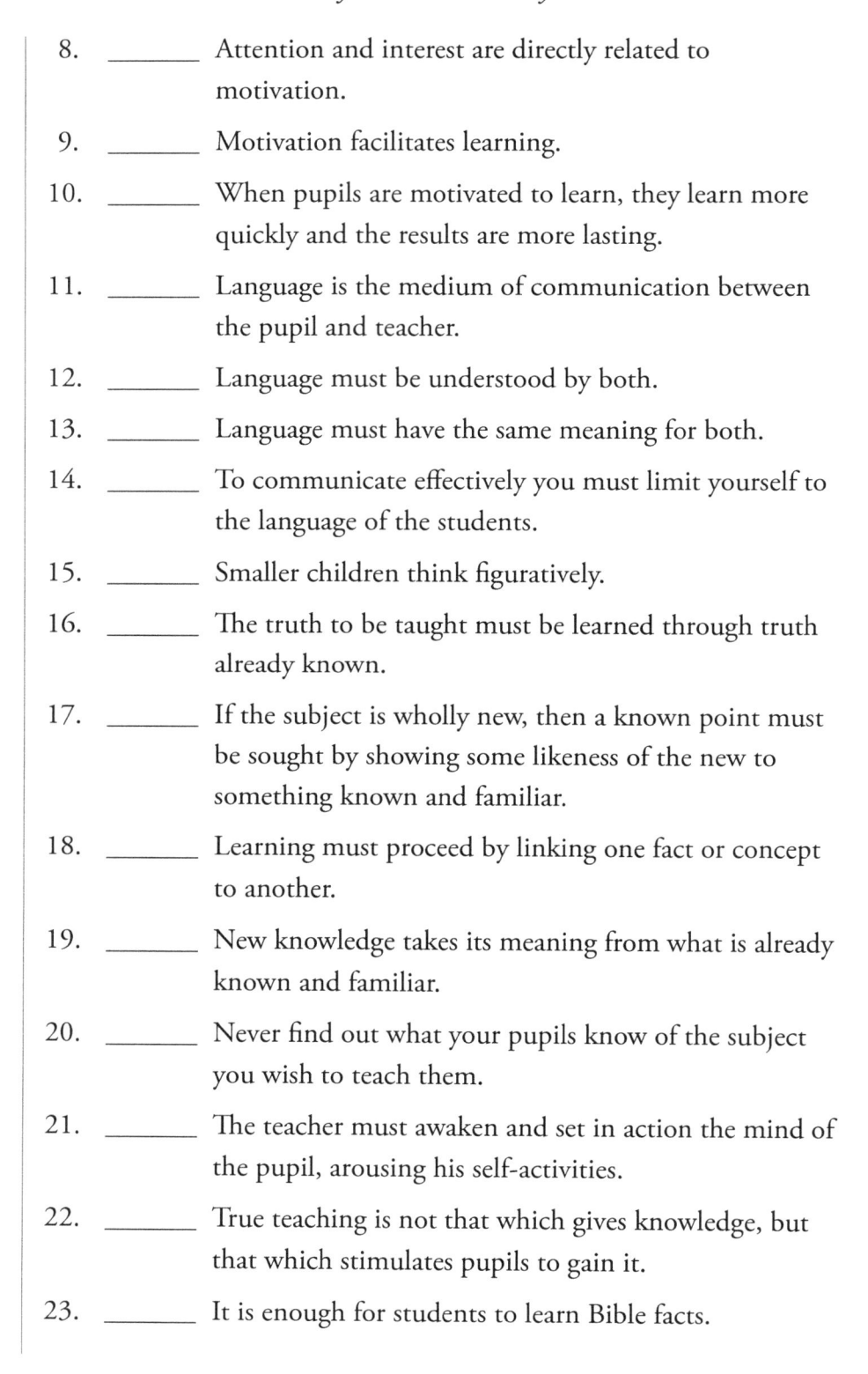

8. _____ Attention and interest are directly related to motivation.

9. _____ Motivation facilitates learning.

10. _____ When pupils are motivated to learn, they learn more quickly and the results are more lasting.

11. _____ Language is the medium of communication between the pupil and teacher.

12. _____ Language must be understood by both.

13. _____ Language must have the same meaning for both.

14. _____ To communicate effectively you must limit yourself to the language of the students.

15. _____ Smaller children think figuratively.

16. _____ The truth to be taught must be learned through truth already known.

17. _____ If the subject is wholly new, then a known point must be sought by showing some likeness of the new to something known and familiar.

18. _____ Learning must proceed by linking one fact or concept to another.

19. _____ New knowledge takes its meaning from what is already known and familiar.

20. _____ Never find out what your pupils know of the subject you wish to teach them.

21. _____ The teacher must awaken and set in action the mind of the pupil, arousing his self-activities.

22. _____ True teaching is not that which gives knowledge, but that which stimulates pupils to gain it.

23. _____ It is enough for students to learn Bible facts.

24. _____ The student must begin to live Bible truths.
25. _____ The learning processes are quickened when students become independent investigators.
26. _____ True learning is not memorization and repetition of the words and ideas of the teacher.
27. _____ The pupil must reproduce in their own minds the truth to be learned.
28. _____ No lesson is fully learned until it is traced to its connections with life.
29. _____ Every fact has its relation to life, and every principle its application.
30. _____ The completion, test and confirmation of the work of teaching must be made by review and application.
31. _____ A review is more than repetition.
32. _____ A repetition by the mind is the rethinking of a thought.
33. _____ A new lesson or a fresh topic always reveals all of itself at first.
34. _____ Frequent repetitions are valuable to correct memorization and aid ready recall.

CHAPTER FIVE
HOW TO PREPARE A LESSON

I. INTRODUCTION

My son was practicing target shooting in the backyard with his B.B. rifle. After he finished shooting, he brought his target in and showed me. Most of the holes were in the center of the target. I asked him how he was able to shoot so many bull's eyes. "It's easy," he replied. "All I do is shoot first, then I draw the target."

Unfortunately, some teachers appear to attempt something similar in their classrooms. They never get around to selecting appropriate lesson goals ahead of time, so they just sort of make things up as they go along. At the end of class, they might even tell you that everything worked out exactly the way they wanted it to! But, whether you're target shooting or teaching, setting goals after the fact doesn't work. Excellent Sunday School teachers plan to achieve certain objectives with their learners, and then they work toward accomplishing those predetermined goals.

This chapter will give a set of steps to follow in order to plan the Sunday School lesson.

II. Step One: Develop a Study Schedule

No rigid prescription can be given for when people should study for their lesson. Some people wake up early and jump out of bed alert with minds ready to function. Others are night owls. They push their minds into second gear and begin to think at 10:00 P.M.

Most teachers do not have one large block of time where they can spend three or four hours studying for the Sunday School lesson. If you are like most Americans, every night is filled with meetings, television programs, or business engagements, in addition to family obligations. Therefore, try to set aside a little time each day to study your Sunday School lesson. You may feel this is asking to much, but should not a Christian spend some time each day alone with God? Why not make the Sunday School lesson one source of personal growth? If God speaks to you through the Scripture portion of the Sunday School curriculum, then it is likely He will speak to your students. A little study each day is better than cramming.

The following outline is suggested at many Sunday School workshops:

- A. Sunday afternoon - Evaluate the day's lesson. Read over the next lesson.
- B. Monday through Wednesday - Study the Bible, using the teacher's manual and other helps.
- C. Thursday through Friday - Write out the actual lesson with aim, method, and materials.
- D. Saturday - Gather material and teaching aids. Review the lesson.
- E. Sunday morning - Review briefly and teach the lesson.

LEARNING EXERCISE #1

INSTRUCTIONS: Fill in the blanks from the section you have just read.

1. No rigid prescription can be given for when people should study for their _____ .

2. Most teachers do not have one large block of _____ where they can spend three or four hours studying for the Sunday School lesson.

3. Teachers should try to set aside a little time _____ _____ to study their Sunday School lesson.

4. If God speaks to you through the Scripture portion of the Sunday School curriculum, then it is likely He will speak to your _____ .

5. A little study each day is better than _____ .

6. Develop a study schedule on a separate sheet of paper.

III. Step Two: Pray For Wisdom

Teachers are not prepared until they prepare themselves through prayer. Prayer preparation means more than walking into the class and asking the pupils to bow their heads. It means more than asking God to bless the time of study and preparation. Elmer Towns lists the following prayers that teachers should pray:

A. Pray for a teachable spirit. One of the first aspects of lesson preparation is to ask God for a teachable spirit. Before we can teach others, we must be taught by the Master Teacher. As teachers approach the Scriptures, they must ask God to guide their study (Psalms 119:18; John 7:17).

B. Pray for the teaching ministry of the Holy Spirit. Too often human teachers see themselves as the only channel in the classroom. Christ promised the Holy Spirit would guide us in all truth. (John 16:13; 14:26) In one sense, the Sunday School has only one teacher, the Holy Spirit. Unless the Holy Spirit works through us, our students will not understand the Bible.

C. Pray for guidance in lesson preparation. Anytime we sit down before the Scriptures for lesson preparation, we should ask God to guide our study. Most Christians habitually ask God's blessing upon food before a meal. In the same manner, teachers should establish the habit of asking God's blessing upon the Word of God when they sit down to study.

D. Pray for each student. Teaching the Word of God is earnest business done for eternity. Teachers attempt to change the destiny of each student. Lost students will be presented with salvation, backslidden pupils will be exhorted to repent, and those who have never left the righteous path will be encouraged to walk closer with their Lord. Teachers must avail themselves of God's power. Teachers should pray for conviction of sin (John 16:1-11), for impact of Scripture (Romans 1:16), and for the moving of the Holy Spirit in student's lives (Acts 1:8).

LEARNING EXERCISE #2

INSTRUCTIONS: Fill in the blanks from the section you have just read.

1. Teachers are not prepared until they prepare themselves through _____ .

2. Prayer preparation means more than walking into the class and asking the _____ to bow their heads.

3. Prayer means more than asking God to bless the time of _____ and _____ .

4. One of the first aspects of lesson preparation is to ask God for a _____ spirit.

5. List the prayers that a teacher should pray:

   a. _____

   b. _____

   c. _____

   d. _____

IV. Step Three: Get an Overview of Lesson Material

A Sunday School class is like one inning of a baseball game. You have to see the whole to appreciate the parts. Just so, every part of the lesson is like a swing of the bat. Before the students can be guided to see the whole, teachers must study and grasp the whole.

Overview is important. At the beginning of a new series, scan all the lessons to gain a total overview. Each lesson is like a spoke in a wheel that completes the cycle of teaching.

Try to visualize the entire series. No lesson of a unit or series can be planned effectively except in the light of its relationship to the rest of the series. The teacher should be entirely familiar with the general content to be taught, its theme, its purpose, and the general method which should be followed in teaching it. Special attention should be given to the lesson preceding and to the one following. The plan should definitely relate the lesson to the previous work of the series.

Since the pupils' experiences do not give them proper perspective or enable them to use recent experience properly in interpreting present situations, the teacher must provide for their conscious recognition of the connection between past and present experiences in order to ensure integrated learning.

LEARNING EXERCISE #3

INSTRUCTIONS: Fill in the blanks from the section you have just read.

1. Before the students can be guided to see the _____ teachers must study and grasp the _____ .

2. Overview is _____ .

3. At the beginning of a new series, a teacher should scan all the lessons to gain a total _____ .

4. The teachers should be entirely familiar with the general content to be taught, its theme, its purpose, and the general method which should be followed in _____ _____ .

5. Special attention should be given to the lesson _____ and to the one _____ .

V. Step Four: Examine the Lesson to be Taught

This is not an intensive study but a preliminary scanning to get a general idea of the content. The teacher should ascertain the purpose of the lesson for the day. The idea of the writer and not the teacher's idea is the important thing, for the office of teachers is to interpret truth, and they cannot do this truly except as they understand the original aim.

This may vary little or much from what the teacher's own purpose for the class is, as determined by the needs of the pupils. If the variation is not too great, supplementation from other sources may be sufficient to bring about adaptation for the present teaching purpose. Whatever is done in this step is done in the light of the teacher's knowledge of the capacities, the interests, and the needs of the pupils.

LEARNING EXERCISE #4

INSTRUCTIONS: Fill in the blanks from the section you have just read.

1. This is not an intensive study but a preliminary scanning to get a general idea of the _____ .

2. The teacher should ascertain the _____ of the lesson.

3. The office of the teacher is to interpret _____ and he cannot do this truly except as he understands the original _____ .

4. If the variation is not too great, _____ from other sources may be sufficient to bring about adaptation for the present teaching purpose.

5. Whatever is done in this step is done in the light of the teacher's knowledge of the capacities, the interests, and the needs of the _____ .

VI. Step Five: Write Out the Aim

The purpose of Sunday School teaching is not only to communicate content but to teach for change. Before you begin to teach, you need to have a clear change in mind that you want the pupils to make.

The aim of a particular lesson will be developed based on the content of the lesson material and according to the students' needs.

The aim should be stated in specific terms, in one or two sentences. It should be a definite statement of the exact thing the teacher would like to accomplish. The aim is the goal of your teaching, its what you want to see happen in your students' lives. Some teachers make the mistake of expecting only a learner's knowledge to change. As a result, they plan their lessons so that learners wind up with a greater accumulation of facts. But the final goal of teaching should be a change in behavior.

While this may seem to be a small matter, stating an aim properly often will have a marked influence on the effectiveness of your teaching. A good aim will help you to target your instruction. A clear teaching aim:

- A. Guides Bible study.
- B. Gives unity, order, and efficiency to teaching.
- C. Gives teachers confidence in the classroom.
- D. Helps teachers use time efficiently.
- E. Helps teachers select teaching aids and methods.
- F. Helps teachers evaluate a lesson.

LEARNING EXERCISE #5

INSTRUCTIONS: Fill in the blanks from the section you have just read.

1. The purpose of Sunday School teaching is not only to communicate content, but to teach for _____ .

2. Before you begin to teach you need to have a clear change in mind that you want the _____ _____ .

3. The aim should be stated in _____ terms, in one or two sentences.

4. The _____ is the goal of your teaching, it's what you want to see happen in your students' lives.

5. List six things a clear teaching aim does:

   a. _____

   b. _____

   c. _____

d. _____

e. _____

f. _____

VII. Step Six: Study the Lesson

To teach the Bible effectively, you need to begin by studying the facts of the Word. Even though you will be using prepared curriculum materials in class, start by studying the biblical facts on which your lesson will be based.

Go to the Bible and familiarize yourself with the appropriate passage. One of the best ways to do this is to read the passage repeatedly. If you begin your lesson preparation early in the week you can review the passage many times during the ensuing days. As you read, write down ideas as they come to you. Later, these concepts or thoughts may be included in your actual lesson.

As you read the passage, ask yourself the following questions and write out your answers:

A. What is the point of the passage?
B. What are the problems in the passage?
C. What parallel passage in Scripture would shed light on this passage?
D. What are some practical applications for the passage?

- After you have studied the passage from the Bible, then consult your teacher's manual. Usually, the teacher's manual explains the lesson content and tells how to teach the lesson. Remember, a teacher's manual cannot make teaching simple or easy. Teaching takes diligence. The teacher's manual was written by competent authorities to make you more effective, not give you an easy time in preparation. You may not always be able to use the manual's suggestions; however, do try to follow them where possible.

- Next, read the student's manual. This is the only material that the pupils will have at their disposal. It is important for you to know what they will experience. Teaching begins "where the students are" and takes them "where they should be."
- There are some resources that are virtually indispensable for Sunday School teachers:

E. Bible concordance - This book lists passages of like meaning in Scripture.

F. Bible dictionary - This reference book gives backgrounds, customs, and geography of Bible lands and meanings of words in Scriptures.

G. Bible commentary - This reference book explains the meaning of verses in the Scriptures.

LEARNING EXERCISE #6

INSTRUCTIONS: Fill in the blanks from the section you have just read.

1. To teach the Bible effectively, you need to begin by studying the facts of the _____ .

2. Even though you will be using prepared curriculum materials in class, _____ by studying the biblical facts on which your lesson will be based.

3. One of the best ways to familiarize yourself with the passage to be taught is by reading the passage _____ .

4. The teacher's manual was written by competent authorities to make you more effective, not give you an _____ time in preparation.

5. Teaching begins "where the students _____ " and takes them where they should _____ ."

6. List three resources that a Sunday School teacher needs:

   a. _____

   b. _____

   c. _____

VIII. Step Seven: Write Out the Lesson Plan

The entire lesson doesn't have to be written out word for word. Organize your Sunday School lesson around an outline. Sunday School teaching is not a written speech that is read to students. Remember, it is Bible study. Try reading a speech or the quarterly and you will drive students from the study of God's Word. Be spontaneous in your presentation. Get the students to discuss topics and ask questions. Interact with them. Points in the outline should be like seeds to be sown, rather than plants in full bloom to be admired.

Include transitional sentences in the lesson outline. These are the hinges that turn the lesson from one point to another. As you finish the introduction and move into your first point, you do not want to lose the students. The introduction captured their attention. Now keep it with a smooth transition.

The following outline can be used to organize your Sunday School lesson.

   A. The aim

   1. This is your objective in the lesson. Express it in a short sentence.

   2. This is what the teacher is trying to accomplish.

   3. This should be the central truth of the lesson and its application.

   4. Refer to it often to be sure that you stay on track in teaching the lesson.

   B. The introduction

   1. A story, picture, object lesson, etc.

2. A discussion of a question.

   3. The purpose is to get the attention of the pupil.

C. The explanation

   1. This is telling the Bible story with its background, setting and customs.

   2. This is interpreting the passage grammatically, historically and geographically.

   3. This must be geared to the pupils learning level.

D. The application

   1. Making the lesson relevant.

   2. Application of the truths and principles of the lesson to life.

   3. The teacher must know the pupils: their age, characteristics, their personal needs, etc., or proper application is not probable.

E. The conclusion

   1. The 'so what' of the lesson

   2. The 'wrap-up'

   3. The aim applied to students' life

   4. You are trying to drive for a decision.

   5. The invitation

LEARNING EXERCISE #7

INSTRUCTIONS: Fill in the blanks from the section you have just read.

1. The entire lesson doesn't have to be written out _____.

2. Organize your Sunday School lesson around an _____.

3. If you read a speech or the quarterly to your students, you will drive them from the _____ of God's Word.

4. The teacher should be spontaneous in their _____.

5. Points in the outline should be like _____ to be sown, rather than _____ in full bloom to be admired.

IX. Step Eight: Write Out Conclusion

Teaching without a conclusion is like fishing without a hook. The fisherman may have the best rod and reel and be a skilled fisherman, yet without a hook, fish cannot be caught. If teachers teach to change lives, then the conclusion secures decisions.

A conclusion is the aim of the Sunday School lesson applied to the life of the student, which results in the student's change.

Some lessons are not concluded, the teacher just stops teaching. Some teachers talk up to the final minute, trying to cram in the last bit of Bible facts. Then they announce, "We'll take up here next Sunday." Such teachers do not conclude, they just finish. They miss both the opportunity to make a change in the students' lives and their greatest opportunity in life (that is, to lead students to Christ).

What about the invitation? Should the teacher in the Sunday School class ask students to close their eyes, bow their heads, and raise their hands to indicate a desire to be saved? Usually no. In small Sunday School classes, teachers should speak personally to each pupil about receiving Christ. However, there may be times when God's Spirit works through open invitations, especially if the class is large and the teacher cannot make a personal contact with each student.

When coming to the conclusion, avoid letting interest lag. You are trying to drive for a decision, and a leisurely approach may allow students' thoughts to wander. Never conclude by apologizing for a poor lesson. If the lesson is poor, the students will know it.

A conclusion should summarize the lesson's main points and refresh the minds of the students. It should be short, personal, pointed, and appropriate.

LEARNING EXERCISE #8

INSTRUCTIONS: Fill in the blanks from the section you have just read.

1. Teaching without a conclusion is like fishing without a _____.

2. If teachers teach to change lives, then the _____ secures decisions.

3. A conclusion is the _____ of the Sunday School lesson, applied to the life of the student, which results in the student's change.

4. Some lessons are not concluded, the teacher just _____ teaching.

5. In small Sunday School classes, teachers should speak _____ to each pupil about receiving Christ.

6. When coming to the conclusion, avoid letting interest _____.

7. Never conclude by _____ for a poor lesson.

8. A conclusion should _____ the lesson's main points and refresh the minds of the students.

X. Step Nine: Write the Introduction

The introduction is the last part of the lesson to be prepared. The purpose of an introduction is to bridge the gap between where the students are and where the lesson begins. You must prepare your lesson before you can bridge the gap from the student to the lesson content.

A good introduction catches the attention of the student, creates a desire to learn, inspires action, and becomes a point of contact. It should promise the students something. However, as with a down payment at a department store, you lose your investment if you do not follow through. Some of the following types of introduction can be used:

    A.   A story from everyday life

    B.   A story from the Scriptures

C. A current event (newspaper clipping)
D. A question
E. A visual aid
F. A filmstrip or slides
G. A quotation from a book or well known personality
H. A picture that reflects the lesson
I. A drawing on the chalkboard

LEARNING EXERCISE #9

INSTRUCTIONS: Fill in the blanks from the section you have just read.

1. The _____ is the last part of the lesson to be prepared.

2. The purpose of an introduction is to _____ _____ _____ between where the students are and where the lesson begins.

3. A good introduction catches the _____ of the student, creates a desire to learn, inspires action, and becomes a point of contact.

4. The introduction should _____ the students something.

5. List four different introductions:

    a. _____

    b. _____

    c. _____

    d. _____

XI. Step Ten: Review and Revise

A good plan is invariably the outcome of at least several revisions. In the revisions the statement of the aim is reconsidered, the outline is reviewed, and the modification of material to be used is made. The technique of teaching that promises to give the best results is subjected to further examination. The wise teacher will give even more consideration to anticipate situations that may arise during the class period, with determination of the possible procedures to be used in meeting them.

Reviewing may also be done a number of times; the teacher will wish to be so familiar with every part and detail of the plan as to be able to use it in the freest way during the teaching period. As a rule, it will be found wise to make a last review just before the class period begins.

LEARNING EERCISE #10

INSTRUCTIONS: Fill in the blanks from the section you have just read.

1. A good plan is invariably the outcome of at least _____ _____ .

2. In the revisions the statement of the aim is reconsidered, the outline is reviewed, and the modification of the _____ to be used is made.

3. The wise teacher will give even more consideration to anticipate situations that may _____ during the class period.

4. Reviewing may also be done a number of _____ .

5. As a rule, it will be found wise to make a _____ _____ just before the class period begins.

CHAPTER REVIEW (For *Certificate of Completion*)

INSTRUCTIONS: Write "T" if the sentence is true, "F" if the sentence is false.

1. _____ No rigid prescription can be given for when people should study for their lesson.

2. _____ Teachers should try to set aside a little time each day to study their Sunday School lesson.

3. _____ A little study each day is better than cramming.

4. _____ Teachers are not prepared until they prepare themselves through prayer.

5. _____ Prayer means just asking God to bless the time of study and preparation.

6. _____ One of the first aspects of lesson preparation is to ask God for a teachable spirit.

7. _____ Before the students can be guided to see the whole, teachers must study and grasp the whole.

8. _____ At the beginning of a new series, a teacher should scan all the lessons to gain a total overview.

9. _____ Special attention should be given to the lesson preceding and to the one following.

10. _____ The office of the teacher is to interpret truth, and he cannot do this truly except as he understands the original aim.

11. _____ The purpose of Sunday School teaching is not only to communicate content, but to teach for change.

12. _____ After you begin to teach you need to have a clear change in mind that you want pupils to make.

13. _____ The aim of the lesson should be stated in specific terms, in one or two sentences.

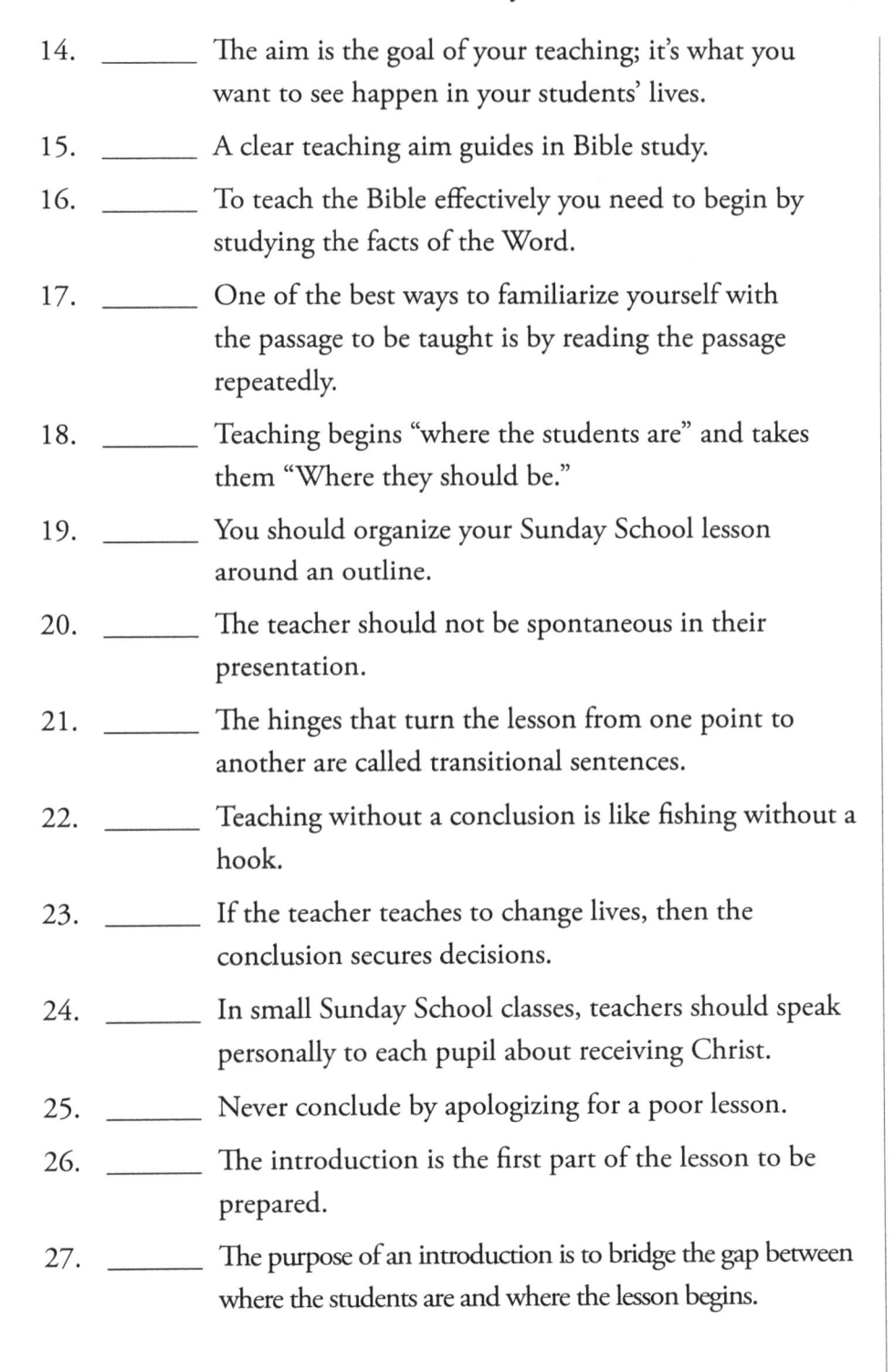

14. _____ The aim is the goal of your teaching; it's what you want to see happen in your students' lives.

15. _____ A clear teaching aim guides in Bible study.

16. _____ To teach the Bible effectively you need to begin by studying the facts of the Word.

17. _____ One of the best ways to familiarize yourself with the passage to be taught is by reading the passage repeatedly.

18. _____ Teaching begins "where the students are" and takes them "Where they should be."

19. _____ You should organize your Sunday School lesson around an outline.

20. _____ The teacher should not be spontaneous in their presentation.

21. _____ The hinges that turn the lesson from one point to another are called transitional sentences.

22. _____ Teaching without a conclusion is like fishing without a hook.

23. _____ If the teacher teaches to change lives, then the conclusion secures decisions.

24. _____ In small Sunday School classes, teachers should speak personally to each pupil about receiving Christ.

25. _____ Never conclude by apologizing for a poor lesson.

26. _____ The introduction is the first part of the lesson to be prepared.

27. _____ The purpose of an introduction is to bridge the gap between where the students are and where the lesson begins.

28. _____ A good introduction catches the attention of the student, creates a desire to learn, inspires action, and becomes a point of contact.

29. _____ The introduction should not promise the students anything.

30. _____ As a rule, it will be found wise to make a last review just before the class period begins.

CHAPTER SIX
HOW TO PRESENT YOUR LESSON

I. Introduction

Suppose that you're planning to entertain guests for dinner. You want this dinner to be something special, so you go to the best supermarket in town. You carefully analyze the contents of product after product, choosing only those which measure up to your high standards. Only the freshest produce will do, and the meat you select is the best cut available. You finally arrive at home with an assortment of the finest ingredients imaginable. You feel satisfied that the evening will be a smashing success.

Shortly before the guests arrive, you get out the largest kettle in your kitchens, set it on the stove, and dump all your purchases into it. As it boils away you anticipate the delight of your guests, knowing that you're about to serve them a dinner of high quality ingredients. At the appointed time, you remove the kettle from the stove, place it on the table, and prepare to watch your guests 'dig in.'

But something is wrong. Your dinner companions don't seem excited. In fact, they appear to have no appetites at all. So you pass the kettle around again. But no one takes a second helping. Before long, your guests graciously excuse themselves and depart. They have been courteous, but cool, and your sense of excitement has waned considerably. How could they reject such fine food? Why did they seem so disinterested when you served them the best ingredients available?

The problem was not your guests' dislike of the ingredients. The problem was in how you presented the meal. Even the most nutritious food must be prepared carefully and presented appropriately to be appreciated. Slopping it all in a kettle just won't do.

The same is true with Sunday School teaching. Many teachers spend sufficient time studying the Bible. They know what God has said, they understand scriptural principles, and they can explain what God expects us to do. But they dump everything into one big kettle; they present their material in a poorly prepared, disorganized manner. Consequently, no one wants seconds (or firsts either).

Really good teachers, however, take time to plan the presentation of their lesson. They know that the presentation is crucial, and they work out that element of their lesson carefully. The teachers have now prepared themselves physically, mentally, and spiritually to teach. They have prepared his lesson throughout the entire week. They have arrived early enough to prepare their pupils. We now come to the climax of the week the teaching of the lesson. This is the purpose of the Sunday School. This is what it is all about. There are several things that are important in presenting the lesson.

II. The Teacher's Appearance When Presenting the Lesson

The key to a teacher's appearance is not to let anything detract from the Sunday School lesson. Anything that would cause a student's attention to be drawn away from the lesson should be eliminated. There are several things in your appearance, while presenting the lesson, that you should pay close attention to:

A. Your Dress

From your head to your toes the same rule applies. Only a comedian may dress eccentrically. Your dress should be modest, conservative, in good taste and suited to the occasion. Simplicity is the keynote of all good design, and that includes clothing.

Dressing conservatively does not mean being colorless or unattractive. On the contrary. It behooves you to be as attractive as you can!

B. Your Grooming

Anyone, expensively dressed or not, can be neatly groomed. It is expected, and justifiably so. Careless grooming will detract from the most carefully prepared and most exquisitely delivered presentation. There are bathtubs, showers, toothbrushes, combs, deodorants, polishes and steam irons. Remember, you are for the moment on exhibition. The aids that keep you nice to be near are numerous. Remember that in speaking your metabolism shoots up; it has the same effect on your body as hard physical exercise. So be nice to look at, nice to be near and be as attractive as you can.

C. Your Posture

It's a little thing, it is true. But life is made up of little things, and success in anything depends on the attention you give to little things, the minor details.

There are a number of things that begin with, or are dependent upon: good posture, your general appearance, your breath control, your voice, to name a few. Good posture means good control of your body.

When you speak or teach on your feet, you need to stand up, not slouched over a table. When you teach from a chair, you need to sit up not slouched forward. And your lungs will have a chance to expand. Many things that are 'right' or 'good for us,' either taste dreadful or make us feel or look odd. This is the exception. You will actually look better. You will look relaxed because you will be relaxed. It is a 'disciplined relaxation,' a result of good control. Good posture means good control.

D. Your Gestures

With your posture under control, there is very little to say about gestures; they will just naturally take care of themselves. The question of *"What will I do with my hands?"* just won't come up.

When you are completely relaxed, when you get to the point where you don't think about them then you may do as you please with them. But, it will be because you want to, not because you don't know what to do with them. Until you reach that point, keep your hands hanging loosely at your sides.

Now when we say 'do with your hands that which comes naturally,' we mean within reason. The restrictions are few and very simple:

1. Don't over-do.

2. Don't become addicted to one gesture.

3. Don't become known for eccentric gestures.

Gestures and posture go together and depend upon and affect each other. When you have mastered the 'disciplined relaxation' that is the result of good control, you will have automatically mastered your gestures also. They will go along with the story, unaffected and unafraid. And you will forget to think, *"What will I do with my hands?"*

E. Your Poise

Poise is not art or studied gestures. It is not imitation. It is not an artificial air put on by a person. It is something infinitely deeper. It is the ability not only to be at ease when things are running smoothly but to keep your head and come up unruffled when things are not.

When you can act at ease, and look at ease, because you are at ease you have poise. It is as simple as that.

LEARNING EXERCISE #1

INSTRUCTIONS: Fill in the blanks from the section you have just read.

1. The key to a teacher's appearance is not to let anything _____ from the Sunday School lesson.

2. Anything that would cause a student's attention to be drawn away from the lesson should be _____.

3. Your dress should be _____, conservative, in good taste, and suited to the occasion.

4. It behooves you to be as _____ as you can!

5. Anyone, expensively dressed or not, can be neatly _____.

6. Careless grooming will detract from the most carefully prepared and most exquisitely _____ presentation.

7. Life is made up of little things, and success in anything depends on the attention you give to _____, the minor details.

8. List three things that depend on good posture.
    a. _____
    b. _____
    c. _____

9. When you teach from a chair you should _____, not slouch forward.

10. With your posture under control, there is very little to say about gestures, they will just _____ take care of themselves.

11. List the restrictions for gestures:
    a. _____
    b. _____
    c. _____

12. _____ and _____ go together and depend upon and affect each other.

13. When you have mastered the 'disciplined relaxation' that is the result of good control, you will have automatically _____ your gestures.

14. _____ is not art or studied gestures.

15. Poise is the ability not only to be at ease when things are running smoothly but to keep your head and come up _____ when things are not.

III. The Teacher's Approach When Presenting the Lesson

The teacher's first sentence may determine the success or failure of the entire lesson. The results that follow depend on the spirit and method of the lesson's introduction. The most carefully made plans avail little if you fail in your approach to the lesson. The first concern is to establish right attitudes and interest among the class members.

Students are motivated in various ways to come to class. Some come because they are brought by parents. Others come out of habit. Many come because they enjoy the fellowship of friends. Probably very few come because they have a sincere desire to study the Word of God.

How do you deal with these attitudes that may range from indifference to outright antagonism? First, establish a point of contact.

Convince the students that you have something to offer that interests them and meets some of their needs. Next, arouse interest in learning. Finally, focus their attention on the lesson. No introduction, regardless of how interesting it may be, is a success if it does not open the door to the lesson.

There are numerous ways to arouse genuine interest. Among these are current events, stories and illustrations, provocative questions, and the use of visuals:

A. Current Events

You may secure attention by referring to some current news. Older students read the newspaper, listen to the radio, and watch television. They have a wide range of interests.

Younger children respond to any event related to their school or play. Teachers who are well informed and keenly interested in the weekday activities of their students should have no difficulty at this point.

B. Stories and Illustrations

A well-told story arouses and sustains attention. A picture or an object gains immediate response. One teacher brought an object lesson for each class in a special box. After a few lessons the students recognized the box and their curiosity was aroused about its contents. To capture their attention all the teacher had to do was to place the box before them on a desk or lectern.

C. Provocative Questions

The questions should be ones which relate directly to the lives of class members and also to the theme of the lesson. Examples of this type question might be:

1. "What would you say if someone asked why you go to church?"
2. "What would you do if you were blamed for something you didn't do?"

D. Visuals

A picture, map, object, filmstrip, or other instructional aid can be used effectively to create interest in the lesson. Students can be drawn into the theme of the lesson by being asked to answer certain questions relating to a map or object that is displayed prior to the class period.

LEARNING EXERCISE #2

INSTRUCTIONS: Fill in the blanks from the section you have just read.

1. The teacher's _____ _____ may determine the success or failure of the entire lesson.

2. The results of the lesson depend on the spirit and method of the lesson's _____ .

3. The most carefully made plans avail little if you fail in your _____ to the lesson.

4. The first concern in presenting the lesson is to establish right _____ and _____ among the class members.

5. List three reasons why students come to Sunday School:
    a. _____
    b. _____
    c. _____

6. List three ways to deal with the different attitudes that may range from indifference to outright antagonism:
    a. _____
    b. _____
    c. _____

7. No introduction, regardless of how interesting it may be, is a _____ if it does not open the door to the lesson.

8. There are numerous ways to arouse genuine interest in the students, list four of them:
    a. _____
    b. _____
    c. _____
    d. _____

IV. The Teacher's Attitude When Presenting the Lesson

There are some basic attitudes that every teacher must possess in presenting a good Bible lesson. These attitudes are not necessarily inborn and they may be attained by prayer and practice.

A. Salesmanship

You must be a good salesman. If you are not absolutely sold on your story, you cannot sell it to others. The 'I don't care attitude' gets an 'I don't care response.' Your listeners will be sold according to the degree you are sold. If your whole attitude says, *"This is an amazing story! It's so good I can hardly wait to tell it!"* then they can hardly wait to hear it. You must be a good salesman.

B Sincerity

Sincerity explains itself. It means without veneer or without a coating; the real thing. You cannot affect sincere delivery. It is an attitude. You have to honestly feel that way. Say what you believe believe what you say without an artificial air. Speak with excitement because you are excited, with sadness because you are sad, with happiness because you are happy. If you are not sincere, you won't fool anyone, especially children. If you are sincere, you won't have to!

C. Earnestness

You must be earnest, especially when your material deals with the Word of God. It means be 'bowed down' with the solemnness of your message.

There are no rules, it is basically an attitude. If you are serious and worshipful about the things of God, you can be joyous, you can be humorous, you can be imaginative, and you will never go beyond the realm of good taste. The Holy Spirit Himself will check you. Somehow, you will know how far you can go. Never be flippant with the Word of God. Be earnest.

D. Whole-heartedness

The teacher must tell the story with whole-heartedness. Give it all you have. If it is worth telling at all, it is worth telling with all your heart.

E. Enthusiasm

Enthusiasm is a trait that is so powerful that it can be downright dangerous if used wrongly. It excites enthusiasm in others, rouses them to respond. It is the sparkplug that sets off dormant action. Enthusiasm is dynamite. It is one of the most powerful weapons a speaker can have.

Enthusiasm does not necessarily mean a lot of noise. You can hiss, roar, fight battles, march and shout, all in a whisper, if the enthusiasm is there. Enthusiasm is an attitude in you that will spark enthusiasm in others, demand a response, and get action. Noisy or quiet, it is a weapon to reckon with.

F. Animation

Animation does not mean that you must jump about like a monkey on a stick. You can be animated standing or sitting still, with your eyes, with your facial expressions, with your gestures, and with your whole being. It is cause and effect; the natural result of whole-heartedness and enthusiasm and being completely sold on your subject.

G. A Broken Heart

A broken heart does not necessarily mean tragedy. If you have a deep personal love for God, a worshipful attitude toward Him, and an immense gratitude for what He has done, your delivery will have the same power to wring a response. Dwight L. Moody had a happy marriage and there was no great tragedy that touched his life, but he could never read the Scriptures without weeping!

H. Be Yourself

This may seem like a paradox, but it is possible to learn all the techniques of dramatics and not feel like you're putting on a show or act. If you absorb them until they are actually a part of you, the result will be complete naturalness. The highest form of art is to banish every obvious trace of it. Be yourself.

LEARNING EXERCISE #3

INSTRUCTIONS: Fill in the blanks from the section you have just read.

1. There are some basic _____ that every teacher must possess in presenting a good Bible lesson.

2. These attitudes are not necessarily inborn and they may be attained by _____ and _____ .

3. List the eight attitudes that a teacher must possess:

   a. _____

   b. _____

   c. _____

   d. _____

   e. _____

   f. _____

   g. _____

   h. _____

4. If you are not absolutely _____ on your story, you cannot _____ it to others.

5. Your listeners will be sold according to the _____ you are sold.

6. If you are not _____ , you won't fool anyone, especially children.

7. You must be _____ especially when your material deals with the Word of God.

8. Never be flippant with the _____ .

9. If a story is worth telling at all, it is worth telling with all your _____ .

10. _____ is a trait that is so powerful that it can be downright dangerous if used wrongly.

How To Present Your Lesson

11. Enthusiasm does not necessarily mean a lot of _____ .

12. _____ does not mean that you must jump about like a monkey on a stick.

13. A broken heart does not necessarily mean _____ .

14. If you have a deep personal love for God, a worshipful attitude toward Him, and an immense gratitude for what He has done, your _____ will have the same power to wring a response.

15. The highest form of _____ is to banish every obvious trace of it. Be yourself!

CHAPTER REVIEW (For *Certificate of Completion*)

INSTRUCTIONS: Write "T" if the sentence is true, "F" if the sentence is false.

1. _____ The key to a teacher's appearance is not to let anything detract from the Sunday School lesson.

2. _____ Anything that would cause a student's attention to be drawn away from the lesson, should be eliminated.

3. _____ Your dress should be modest, conservative, in good taste, and suited to the occasion.

4. _____ It behooves you to be as attractive as you can.

5. _____ Careless grooming will add to a carefully prepared and most exquisitely delivered presentation.

6. _____ When you teach from a chair you should sit up not slouch forward.

7. _____ With your posture under control, there is very little to say about gestures, they will just naturally take care of themselves.

8. _____ When you have mastered the 'disciplined relaxation,' that is the result of good control, you will have automatically mastered your posture.

9. _____ Poise is the ability, not only to be at ease when things are running smoothly, but to keep your head and come up unruffled when things are not.

10. _____ The teacher's first sentence may determine the success or failure of the entire lesson.

11. _____ The results of the lesson depend on the spirit and method of the lesson introduction.

12. _____ The most carefully made plans avail little if you fail in your approach to the lesson.

13. _____ The first concern in presenting the lesson is to establish right attitudes and interest among the class members.

14. _____ No introduction, regardless of how interesting it may be, is a success if it does not open the door to the lesson.

15. _____ Some of the ways to arouse a genuine interest in the students are: current events, stories and illustrations, provocative questions and visuals.

16. _____ There are some basic attitudes that every teacher must possess in presenting a good Bible lesson.

17. _____ Attitudes to help present a good lesson are inborn.

18. _____ You don't have to be sold on your story to make others sold on it.

19. _____ Your listeners will be sold according to the degree you are sold.

20. _____ If you are not sincere, you won't fool anyone, especially children.

21. _____ You must be earnest, especially when your material deals with the Word of God.

22. _____ If a story is worth telling at all, it is worth telling with all your heart.

23. _____ Enthusiasm is a trait that is so powerful that it can be downright dangerous if used wrongly.

24. _____ A broken heart means there must be tragedy.

25. _____ Enthusiasm does not necessarily mean a lot of noise.

CHAPTER SEVEN
HOW TO USE DIFFERENT TEACHING METHODS AND AIDS

I. INTRODUCTION

A well known preacher and Sunday School expert took me out to lunch one day. Halfway through the meal he looked at me and asked, *"What are these people at the table to the right of us talking about?"* I replied that I had no idea. Then he asked, *"Well what are these people at the table to the left of us talking about?"* Again, I replied that I had no idea. A third time he asked me, *"What are these people at the table behind us talking about?"* For a third time I replied that I had no idea. He then said, *"I just demonstrated to you the basis of the principle of the **Guided Discovery Learning Bible Study**."* Then he explained how it works.

- A. First, it is departmentalized by age and gender.

- B. Secondly, the departments are broken into classes of less than fifteen.

- C. Thirdly, each class sits around a table with their teacher.

- D. Finally, all of the classes are placed in an open room, as in the restaurant. If he hadn't proved it to me I never would have believed it. We get used to doing things one way and resist any kind of change.

- E. There are basically two philosophies in teaching a Sunday School class:

    1. The Master Teacher Approach is teacher-centered, relying mainly on the lecture method of teaching. The Sunday School classes are generally large (16 or more). The teacher stands in front of the class, behind a lectern, and lectures using few if any other teaching methods. The students sit quietly listening. The teacher seeks limited participation from the students.

    2. The Guided Discovery Learning approach to teaching a Sunday School is a student centered method. This is

the approach Sunday School experts promote as best suited for student learning. This chapter explains how to lead a Guided Discovery Learning Bible Study.

II. It Is Important to Get the Proper Mental Picture of What We Will Be Doing In Our Sunday School.

Put out of your mind the picture of a Sunday School class of twenty to fifty people, and you standing behind a lectern delivering a 'message' to the class. Do not use a lectern or a pulpit in a class. Sit with your pupils. This is the best way to teach all the way through to adults if conditions will permit you to do so. It is nearly impossible for a preacher to 'teach' if he is standing up behind a lectern. Sitting down causes one to hold his voice down, and allows a more personal eye to eye contact.

You will have six to ten people out of your enrollment of thirteen to twenty meeting together. After an assembly of fifteen to twenty minutes with the rest of the Sunday School or your department, you will meet with your class around a table.

    A.   The process you will use in teaching is called Guided Discovery Learning. Guided Discovery Learning, as the name implies, focuses on the teacher guiding the class, rather than preaching to the class or lecturing the entire session.

    B.   Guided Discovery Learning encourages participation of the class members. It is based upon the presupposition that people learn more through 'hearing and doing' together than through simply 'hearing.' The data on which Guided Discovery Learning is based on sound educational data. First, notice how we learn:

        1.   We learn 83 percent of what we know through sight.

        2.   We learn 11 percent of what we know through hearing.

        3.   We learn 32 percent of what we know through smell.

        4.   We learn 12 percent of what we know through touch.

        5.   We learn 1 percent of what we know through taste.

C. Secondly, notice how we retain:
1. We retain 10 percent of what we read.
2. We retain 20 percent of what we hear.
3. We retain 30 percent of what we see.
4. We retain 50 percent of what we see and hear.
5. We retain 70 percent of what we say.
6. We retain 90 percent of what we see, say, and do.

Therefore, a good teacher will spend no more than 50-60 percent of the time talking. The other part of the time will be spent in class participation.

D. The question is the most basic tool of Guided Discovery Learning. The teacher asks questions of the group, requiring the individual to think, read, study, ponder, and reason. When the group responds, the teacher expands, develops, enlarges, and illustrates the point. This was the method of Christ if you study the gospels.

E. In Guided Discovery Learning, discussion is an important technique; however, it is not 'open' discussion where you are soliciting everyone's opinion. Remember, this is guided learning, as the teacher you are a guide, a facilitator, a leader. It is your responsibility to keep the class on track toward your specific objective (which is the lesson aim). This is why there was much time spent on how to prepare your lesson. Your outline (aim, introduction, explanation, application, illustration, and conclusion) is what you will use to keep the discussion on track.

LEARNING EXERCISE #1

INSTRUCTIONS: Fill in the blanks from the section you have just read.

1. The MasterTeacher approach is _____ - _____ relying mainly on the lecture method of teaching.

2. The Guided Discovery Learning approach to teaching a Sunday School is a _____ - _____ method.

3. Sitting down when teaching causes one to hold his voice down, and allows a more _____ eye to eye contact.

4. Guided Discovery Learning, as the name implies, focuses on the teacher _____ the class, rather than _____ to the class or lecturing the entire session.

5. Guided Discovery Learning encourages participation of the class _____ .

6. Guided Discovery Learning is based upon the presupposition that people learn more through _____ and _____ together than through simply hearing.

7. We retain _____ of what we see, say, and do.

8. A good teacher will spend no more than _____ of the time talking.

9. The other part of the time will be spent in class _____ .

10. The _____ is the most basic tool of Guided Discovery Learning.

11. When a teacher asks a question of a group it requires the individual to do what five things?

    a.

    b.

    c.

    d.

    e.

12. What is the teaching method that Christ used, seen in the Gospels? _____ _____ .

13. In Guided Discovery Learning, discussion is an important technique: however, it is not 'open' discussion where you are soliciting every one's _____ .

14. It is your responsibility to keep the class on track toward your specific _____ .

15. Your _____ is what you will use to keep the discussion on track.

III. Teaching Method Available In the Master Teacher Approach

A. Lecture

Lecturing is the most widely used teaching method, especially at the adult, young adult, and sometimes high school level. In this method, the teacher speaks to the class, giving the information to be learned.

    1. Use the lecture method:
        a. When giving information
        b. When the learners are already motivated
        c. When the speaker is skilled in using word pictures
        d. When the group is too large for other methods to be used
        e. When adding to or stressing what the learner has read
        f. When reviewing or previewing a lesson or activity
        g. When pupils can understand the words used
        h. When used a few minutes at a time followed by questions and answers, discussion etc.
        i. When using visuals

B. The advantages and limitations of the lecture method:
  1. Advantages
     a. Can be used with adults
     b. Conserves time
     c. Can be used with large groups
     d. Involves use of very few aids
     e. Can be used to add to what has been read
     f. Can be used to review and preview lessons or activities
  2. Limitations
     a. Prevents the learner from responding
     b. Few lecturers are good speakers
     c. Can become uninteresting
     d. Lecturer can take advantage of listeners
     e. Is difficult to use with children
     f. Limits retention
     g. Usually makes use of only one sense
     h. Speakers cannot always judge the reactions of the learners.

III. Teaching methods available in the Guided Discovery Learning Approach

  A. Group Discussion
     1. Group discussion is a guided period of thought and opinion designed to move learners to a stated objective (aim) in which the leader and the learners:
        a. Share ideas
        b. Identify problems
        c. Find solutions

How To Use Different Teaching Methods and Aids   83

2. Use the group discussion method:
   a. When sharing ideas
   b. To stimulate interest in problems
   c. To help members express their ideas
   d. To identify and explore a problem
   e. To create an informal atmosphere
   f. To get opinions from persons who hesitate to speak
3. The advantages of the group discussion method:
   a. Provides for sharing
   b. Is democratic in approach
   c. Encourages togetherness among members
   d. Broadens viewpoints
   e. Provides opportunities
   f. Helps develop leadership skills
4. The limitations of the group discussion method:
   a. Cannot be used with large groups
   b. Members may have limited information
   c. Discussion is easily side-tracked
   d. Requires skilled leadership
   e. Talkative persons may dominate
   f. Most people require a more formal approach

B.   Questions and Answers

In the questions and answer method, the teacher has a set of prepared questions that help to lead the students to the aim of the lesson.

1. Use the question and answers:
   a. At any point in a lesson
   b. With other teaching methods
   c. In written form on the board, on a poster, or on individual copies

d. With sentences beginning with How?, Which? and Why?

e. Allowing thinking timet for people before asking for a response.

2. The advantages of the question and answer method:

a. Questions guide the teacher because they provide 'feedback'.

b. Questions involve everyone if not asked to a specific person.

c. Questions are a great way to get people to evaluate.

3. The limitations of the question and answer method:

a. If questions are poorly planned and only require one word answers, they will bring discussion and follow-up to an end.

b. If the question is asked to a specific person, others quit thinking.

C. Brainstorming

Brainstorming is a method of problem solving in which group members suggest in rapid fire order all the possible solutions they can think of. Criticism is ruled out. Evaluation of ideas comes later.

1. Use the brainstorming method:

a. To encourage creative thinking

b. To encourage participation

c. When determining possible solutions to problems

d. In connection with other methods

e. To encourage presentation of new ideas

f. To create a warm, friendly feeling in the group

g. The advantages of the brainstorming method:

h. Encourages new ideas

i. Encourages all members to take part

j. Produces a 'chain reaction' of ideas

k. Does not take a great deal of time

l. Can be used with large or small groups

m. Does not require highly skilled leadership

n. Requires little equipment

o. The limitations of the brainstorming method

p. Can easily get out of hand

q. Evaluation must follow if method is to be effective

r. Members are slow to understand that any idea is acceptable

s. Members tend to begin evaluation when an idea is suggested

B. The Case Study

A case study is an account of a problem situation, including sufficient detail to make it possible for groups to analyze problems involved. The case is a 'slice of life' that invites diagnosis, prescription and possible treatment. It may be presented in writing, orally, dramatically, on film, or as a recording.

1. Use the case study method:

    a. When relating a problem to life situations

    b. When analyzing a problem

    c. When members do not have the ability to role play

    d. To help members identify with a problem

    e. When possible solutions are desired

    f. When analyzing the bearing of facts upon a problem

2.. The advantages of the case study method:

    a. May be written, filmed, recorded, acted out, or told as a story

    b. May be assigned for study before discussion

      c. Provides equal opportunity for members to suggest solutions

      d. Creates the atmosphere for the exchange of ideas

      e. Deals with problems related to life

      f. Provides opportunity to apply insights and skills

      g. Provides a type of simulated follow through

C. Role Playing

Role playing is the unrehearsed, dramatic enactment of a human conflict situation by two or more persons for the purpose of analysis by the group.

  1. Use role playing method:

      a. When members need to increase their understanding of opposing points of view

      b. When group members have the ability to use the method

      c. When helping members to identify with a problem

      d. When trying to change attitudes

      e. When involvement of emotions aids in presenting the problem

      f. When creating the stage for problem solving

      g. The advantages of role playing

      h. Gains immediate interest

      i. May be used with groups of all sizes

      j. Helps members analyze situations

      k. Increases self-confidence of members

      l. Helps members identify themselves with a problem

      m. Helps members experience the other person's point of view

      n. Creates the stage for problem solving

2. The limitations of role playing:
    a. Members may identify participants with the problems
    b. Most members are reluctant to role playing
    c. Requires trained leadership
    d. Limited in number of situations in which it can be used
    e. Role players may have difficulty releasing their roles

D. Buzz Groups

Buzz groups are small study groups of a large group. The groups discuss assigned problems, usually for the purpose of reporting back to the larger group.

1. Use buzz groups:
    a. When the group is too large for all members to take part
    b. When exploring various facets of a subject
    c. When some group members are slow to take part
    d. When time is limited
    e. To create a warm, friendly feeling in the group
2. The advantages of buzz groups:
    a. Encourages the timid members
    b. Creates a warm, friendly feeling
    c. Provides for sharing of leadership
    d. Saves time
    e. Develops leadership skills
    f. Provides for pooling of ideas
    g. May be used easily with other methods
    h. Provides variety

3. The limitations of buzz groups:
    a. May result in pooling of ignorance
    b. Groups may 'chase rabbits'
    c. Leadership may be poor
    d. Reports may not be very well organized
    e. Requires study beforehand if reliable conclusions are reached
    f. May result in temporary cliques
    g. Usually takes time to arrange equipment for use by small groups

LEARNING EXERCISE #2

INSTRUCTIONS: Fill in the blanks from the section you have just read.

1. _____ is the most widely used teaching method. In this method, the teacher speaks to the class, giving the information to be learned.

2. _____ is a guided period of thought and opinion designed to move learners to a stated objective.

3. List the three things the leader and the learners do in group discussion:

    a. _____

    b. _____

    c. _____

4. In the question and answer method, the teacher has a set of _____ that help to lead the students to the aim of the lesson.

5. Brainstorming is a method of problem solving in which group members suggest in rapid fire order all the _____ _____ they can think of.

6. A case study is an account of a problem situation, including sufficient detail to make it possible for groups to _____ involved.

7. The _____ is a 'slice of life' that invites diagnosis, prescription and possible treatment.

8. _____ _____ is the unrehearsed, dramatic enactment of a human conflict situation by two or more persons for the purpose of analysis by the group.

9. Buzz groups are small study _____ of a large group.

10. Buzz groups discuss assigned problems, usually for the purpose of reporting back to the larger _____ .

IV. Suggestions In Using Guided Discovery Learning

A. How to stay on track with your class

1. If a question is relevant at the point in the lesson when asked, answer it. Spend as much time as you feel is necessary.

2. If for some reason a question is not relevant, use the following techniques:

    a. Postpone - answer at the end of the lesson

    b. Preclude - as you study, there are questions that you will anticipate. If you do not wish for them to come up, pose them prior to anyone else having a chance to ask them, and then answer them yourself.

    c. Promptly answer - answer the question quickly, then get on with the lesson

    d. Promise to research and return later with the answer

A great fear of new teachers, especially working with adults is, *"What if they ask a question to which you don't know the answer?"* Simply say, *"I don't know, but I'll find out and tell you next week."* Admitting you do not know is often a great asset. It gives you a genuineness that people respect. No one knows everything, so pride should not keep you from admitting that you do not know.

    B.   Some things you should **never** do in class

        1.   Do not call on a specific person to pray without first having asked their permission. Illustration: *"John, may I call on you to pray in our class?"*

        2.   Do not ask direct questions. Do not say, *"Bob, what did Jesus say in verse 10?"* Instead, say, *"Class, what did Jesus say in verse 10?"* In other words do not put people on the spot to where there could be potential embarrassment. Remember, some people cannot read and will always hide this. Do not 'unmask' them. One suggestion here is that you might call a faithful member at home and have them prepared for a specific question, particularly if the question involves rather detailed study.

        3.   Do not ask a visitor a question or to read; however, if they volunteer, encourage their participation. This will make them feel a part of the class.

    C.   How do you handle the person who wants to dominate the class?

        1.   First, teach your regular class members how we want our classes to be conducted. Tell them you strongly encourage their participation, however, you do not want anyone person to dominate the discussions. They are to participate in Guided Discovery Learning.

        2.   If a person becomes disruptive to the class, you will ultimately have to tell them privately after a class session, that they must give others an opportunity to participate. This will call for strong leadership. Ask for directions from your departmental director before undertaking this.

D. Summary

   1. Understand what Guided Discovery Learning is and the importance of your preparation, and study the various teaching methods outlined here. Keep this lesson, and each time you prepare your lesson, review the methods and plans on how you will use several or all of these in your Bible study.

   2. Remember do not preach! People learn much more through participation than through listening alone. Try to involve every class member at every available opportunity. You make it easier to learn, you encourage their participation. Involvement creates relationships, relationships bind people to a church and a Bible study ministry.

LEARNING EXERCISE #3

INSTRUCTIONS: Fill in the blanks from the section you have just read.

1. If a questions is _____ at the point in the lesson when asked, answer it.

2. List four techniques that you should use if irrelevant questions are asked:

   a. _____

   b. _____

   c. _____

   d. _____

3. A great fear of new teachers, especially working with adults is, *"What if they ask a question to which I don't know the* _____ *?"*

4. What should you say if somebody asks a question and you don't know the answer? _____ _____ .

5. No one knows _____ .

6. List three things you must never do:

   a. _____

   b. _____

   c. _____

7. Teach your regular class members how we want our classes to be _____ .

8. If a person becomes disruptive to the class, you will ultimately have to tell them _____ after a class session they must give others an opportunity to participate.

9. _____ for direction from your departmental director before undertaking this.

10. Keep this lesson, and each time you prepare your lesson, review the methods and plans on how you will use several or all of these in your _____ .

11. Try to involve _____ class member at every available opportunity.

12. Involvement creates relationships; relationships bind people to a _____ and a _____ ministry.

VI. The Learning Aids

   A. A learning aid is any device that helps teachers communicate more effectively with their students. An aid may help impart knowledge, attitudes, skills, or understanding; arouse emotions; or develop appreciation. A learning aid, therefore, is a tool for improving instruction.

B. Learning aids are valuable for several reasons.

   1. First, they help overcome the language barrier in teaching. Most teaching is verbal, either written or oral; yet increasingly our culture emphasizes visual learning.

   2. Aids help capture and hold student attention, and make learning more rapid, thus making more efficient use of class time.

   3. Students remember longer what they have learned when reinforced by visual aids. Aids can make the Bible come alive in ways that words alone cannot.

C. If all of these things are true about learning aids, why don't more teachers use them?

   1. Perhaps the main obstacle is habit; we use only what is most comfortable and familiar.

   2. Also, aids, usually take extra time and planning to prepare and require certain skills in using equipment.

   3. Many aids, especially audiovisuals, do involve some expense for equipment and materials. Yet, when you come to realize how effective these aids may be, you will quickly forget these obstacles.

D. Remember that no learning aid is of itself either effective or ineffective, the learning aid depends on the skill of the leader. The following list of learning aids is not exhaustive:

   1. Records
   2. Tapes
   3. Objects and models
   4. Maps and globes
   5. Pictures
   6. Bulletin boards
   7. Chalkboard
   8. Flip chart
   9. Flannel graph

10. Puppets
11. Films
12. Filmstrips and slides
13. Transparencies
14. Videocassettes
15. Student activity books
16. Handcraft
17. Pin-board chart
18. Slip chart

LEARNING EXERCISE #4

INSTRUCTIONS: Fill in the blanks from the section you have just read.

1. A _____ is any device that helps teachers communicate more effectively with their students.

2. A learning aid, therefore, is a tool for improving _____ .

3. Learning aids help overcome the _____ _____ in teaching.

4. Aids help capture and hold students' _____ and make _____ U more rapid thus making more efficient use of class time.

5. Learning aids can make the Bible come _____ in ways that words alone cannot.

6. List three reasons why more teachers don't use learning aids:

   a. _____

   b. _____

   c. _____

7. Remember that no learning aid is of itself either _____ or _____ , the learning aid depends on the _____ of the teacher.

CHAPTER REVIEW (For *Certificate of Completion*)
Instructions: Write 'T" if the sentence is true, 'F" if the sentence is false.

1. _____ The Master-Teacher approach is teacher-centered, relying mainly on the lecture method of teaching.

2. _____ The Guided Discovery Learning approach to teaching a Sunday School is a student-centered method.

3. _____ Sitting down when teaching causes one to hold his voice down, and allows a more personal eye to eye contact.

4. _____ Guided Discovery Learning, as the name implies, focuses on the teacher preaching to the class, rather than guiding the class.

5. _____ Guided Discovery Learning encourages participation.

6. _____ Guided Discovery Learning is based upon the presupposition that people learn more through hearing and doing together than through simply hearing.

7. _____ A good teacher will spend no more than 50-60 percent of the time talking.

8. _____ The question is the most basic tool of Guided Discovery Learning.

9. _____ It is the students' responsibility to keep the class on track toward your specific objective.

10. _____ Your outline is what you will use to keep the discussion on track.

11. _____ Lecturing is the most widely used teaching method.

12. _____ Group discussion is a guided period of thought and opinion designed to move learners to a stated objective.

13. _____ Brainstorming is a method of problem solving in which group members suggest in rapid fire order all the possible solutions they can think of.

14. _____ A case study is an account of a problem situation, including sufficient detail to make it possible for groups to analyze problems involved.

15. _____ Role playing is the rehearsed, dramatic enactment of a human conflict situation by two or more persons for the purpose of analysis by the group.

16. _____ Buzz groups discuss assigned problems, usually for the purpose of reporting back to the larger group.

17. _____ A great fear of new teachers, especially working with adults is, *"What if they ask a question to which I don't know the answer?"*

18. _____ Teach your regular class members how we want our classes to be conducted.

19. _____ If a person becomes disruptive to the class, you will ultimately have to tell them privately after a class session they must give others an opportunity to participate.

20. _____ A learning aid is any device that helps teachers communicate more effectively with their students.

21. _____ A learning aid is a tool for improving instruction.

22. _____ Learning aids help overcome the language barrier.

23. _____ Aids help capture and hold students' attention and make learning more rapid.

24. _____ No learning aid is of itself either effective or ineffective, the learning aid depends on the skill of the teacher.

CHAPTER EIGHT
HOW TO RELATE TO YOUR STUDENTS

I. Introduction

Sometime ago a pastor asked a teacher how his Sunday School class was progressing. 'I wish I knew," he replied.

- A. My students never say anything. They just sit there and stare at me. *Sometimes, I feel as though I'm teaching the Great Stone Face."*
- B. The "Great Stone Face" to which he referred is a geologic formation found in the mountains of New England. Gazing at this stone resemblance of a man's profile can be a delightful experience. But, when the students you're teaching are totally unresponsive, looking at stone faces is anything but enjoyable.

Another teacher described similar feelings. One Sunday, he felt he was really communicating with his students; every eye in the room was riveted on him. Wow, he thought, *"Do I ever have their attention!"* But as he moved off to one side of his lectern he noticed that every eye was still focused on the same spot. They were staring, glassy eyed, at nothing. The Great Stone Face had struck again!

- C. It doesn't have to be that way. We don't need to endure the agony of thinking or fearing that we may be boring our students. Of course, we who teach children casually know immediately when they get bored. When children become bored, they tune out the teacher and start doing something else.
- D. Older youths and adults usually are different. Most of them have learned to be polite when they get bored. So they just sit there quietly and courteously. The teacher must be observant enough to recognize what is happening (or more accurately, not happening).
- E. The teacher must be able to relate on the student's level that they are teaching. Understanding the characteristics of the

group or class that you are teaching, will help you to relate to them.

II. Two and Three Year-Olds

A. Physically

1. They are active; provide many opportunities for them to move about and exercise their large muscles.
2. They can use their hands; let them do their own table work.
3. They are gaining coordination; encourage them do things for themselves such as working puzzles, building and coloring.
4. They have short endurance; give them a rest time and plan quiet activities during the day.
5. Their voices are still developing; sing simple, short-range melodies with easy words.
6. They like to imitate; do the things you want them to learn.

B. Mentally

1. They are inquisitive; let them touch things, and cheerfully and truthfully answer their questions.
2. They can learn; teach them the Bible on their own level.
3. They have a short attention span; provide a variety of short stories and activities and keep the program moving.
4. They believe their teacher; tell them the truth.
5. They have a poor memory; constantly repeat and review the Bible verse and theme during various activities.
6. They think in small numbers; give them one thing to do at a time.

7. They do not understand symbolism; avoid use of songs, stories and rhymes that use symbolism.
8. Use simple words and show them what they mean.
9. They use their senses; provide things they can hear, see, smell, taste and touch.
10. They like repetition; provide varied activities during which you continually repeat the theme and action expected.

C. Emotionally
1. They are fearful; keep the same room, equipment and teachers as much as possible.
2. They respond to love; take time to give them a pat or a hug or to read them a story.
3. They need security; gently enforce behavioral limits.
4. They need acceptance; praise their good behavior and their efforts.
5. They are sensitive; keep the class orderly and maintain a cheerful spirit.
6. They say 'no'; you should use positive remarks, not questions.

D. Socially
1. They are dependent; be readily available when they want or need help.
2. They are self-centered; direct them to be thankful and to share.
3. They play alone; let them play by themselves and do not force interaction with other children.
4. They like friends; even imaginary ones, play and pretend with them as you direct their thoughts toward the aims of the lesson.
5. They need attention; notice them and bend down to talk to them.

E. **Spiritually**
   1. They want to pray; encourage them to talk to God anytime.
   2. They are interested in the Bible; teach them to love and respect it.
   3. They want to know about God; teach them God loves them.
   4. They sense the wonders of God; help them learn about creation and thank God for it.
   5. They are usually not ready to receive Christ as Savior; do not explain the plan of salvation in detail to a two or three-year-old child because they are unable to understand all of these truths. Do, however, teach them some basic facts about God and Jesus, which provides a foundation for accepting Christ in the years to come.

LEARNING EXERCISE #1

INSTRUCTIONS: Fill in the blanks from the section you have just read.

1. Describe six physical characteristics of a two or three-year-old:
   a. _____
   b. _____
   c. _____
   d. _____
   e. _____
   f. _____

2. List nine mental characteristics of a two or three-year-old:
   a. _____
   b. _____
   c. _____
   d. _____
   e. _____

f. _____
g. _____
h. _____
i. _____

3. List six emotional characteristics of a two or three-year-old:

    a. _____
    b. _____
    c. _____
    d. _____
    e. _____
    f. _____

4. List five social characteristics of a two or three-year-old:

    a. _____
    b. _____
    c. _____
    d. _____
    e. _____

5. List five spiritual characteristics of a two or three-year-old:

    a. _____
    b. _____
    c. _____
    d. _____
    e. _____
    f. _____

III. Four and Five-Year-Olds

A. Physically

1. The four or five-year-old child is growing rapidly and seems to have boundless energy. They are getting greater control of their muscles.

2. Because of their energy, they need a variety of activities, as well as several changes during the class period. They enjoy acting out a Bible story.

3. Use large crayons for the younger child. Small crayons may be used by the older child. Allow them to be a helper, when possible, by letting them pass out such things as crayons and paper.

4. Since they become tired easily, the activities should vary between active and quiet ones.

B. Mentally

1. The four or five-year-old child's attention span is increasing. They are able to sit five to fifteen minutes, depending upon the activity. They are more interested in doing than in talking or listening.

2. A child of this age loves to ask questions, especially "What" and "Where." They are very curious. They forget easily and may ask the same question over and over. They may ask questions or tell something not related to the lesson. However, do not ignore their questions, because they acquire a great deal of knowledge through their questioning.

3. The child's vocabulary is increasing, and they speak in simple sentences. Use words and concepts they can understand.

4. They like to use their imagination. This is valuable during story time, for it helps them become a part of the story. However, they cannot always tell the difference between truth and fantasy. Therefore, tell them plainly what is fantasy.

5. They learn through imitation. Set good examples before them both in your stories and in your personal life.

C. Emotionally

1. The four or five-year-old child has intense emotions that can be easily upset. He may have sudden outbursts of anger. Control this by having a calm atmosphere in the classroom, being calm yourself and avoiding abrupt endings to their activities.
2. Though they are growing up, they still have some fears. Some children may not be used to being away from their mothers and fathers.
3. The four or five-year-old child may cry when he does not get his way. He needs to be taught to ask for things instead of crying or whining.
4. They desire approval and sympathy from their teacher. Therefore, find something for which to praise each child.

D. Socially

1. The four or five-year-old child enjoys playing with other children. They are learning to share and to take turns. Put the children in small groups so their turns come often.
2. The child is self-centered at this age. Encourage them to share and to consider others more important than themselves.

F. Spiritually

1. The four or five-year-old child thinks of God in a personal way. They understand God loves and cares for them. Help them realize Jesus is God's Son.
2. They understand the difference between doing right and doing wrong. They need to understand that doing wrong is sin and does not please God. Teach them Jesus died for these sins and wants to be their Savior. Teach them also that they must believe on Jesus as their Savior.

3. They can understand the Bible is God's special Book. Tell them that the stories in the Bible are real and not make believe.

4. Some four or five-year-old children may be ready to accept Christ as their Savior. However, many are not. **Never push a child into a decision.**

LEARNING EXERCISE #2

INSTRUCTIONS: Fill in the blanks from the section you have just read.

1. The four or five-year-old child is growing rapidly and seems to have _____ energy.

2. They enjoy acting out a _____ .

3. Use large _____ for the younger child.

4. Since they becomes tired easily, the activities should vary between _____ and _____ ones.

5. List five mental characteristics of a four or five-year-old:

    a. _____

    b. _____

    c. _____

    d. _____

    e. _____

6. The four or five-year-old child has intense emotions that can be _____ .

7. Control this by having a _____ atmosphere in the classroom, being _____ yourself and avoiding _____ endings to their activities.

8. Some children may not be used to being away from their _____ and _____ .

9. The four or five-year-old child may cry when he does not get his _____ .

10. They desire _____ and _____ from his teacher.

11. List two social characteristics of a four or five-year-old:

    a. _____

    b. _____

12. List four spiritual characteristics of a four or five-year-old:

    a. _____

    b. _____

    c. _____

    d. _____

IV. First, Second and Third Grade - 6, 7, and 8-Year-Olds

A. Physically

1. The children seem much taller and thinner than preschool children, and there are a few toothless smiles scattered throughout the group.

2. These children are constantly on the move. They love to work hard and to play hard. It's good to have a recreation period to provide strenuous activities in which all the children can participate at one time.

3. In the classroom the children can participate by memorizing Scripture, by writing and coloring in their workbook and by making craft projects.

B. Mentally

1. They are learning to read and write, and they are eager to exercise these newly acquired abilities. The older children may be able to read cursive, but you should always use primary script.

2. These children have good memories, so emphasize Scripture memorization. To make this time enjoyable, use various methods. They like to play games that use words and numbers, so they will enjoy the hidden messages in puzzles.

3. Their attention span is longer than preschoolers', but they need variety in the program. Make use of songs, visuals, and puppets.

4. They are beginning to reason and to form some of their own conclusions. The applications in the Bible lessons should be geared to give the children opportunity for input, but you still need to guide them.

5, They have good imaginations, are able to distinguish between fact and fancy and are literal-minded. When life-related stories are fictitious, let the children know.

6. Avoid symbolism in your songs and your teaching.

C. Emotionally

1. These children are impatient and easily excited. Be patient and calm yourself, and provide a cheerful and calm atmosphere in the classroom.

2. During recreation time the children may be allowed more freedom, but even here the leaders should be in control.

3. Sometimes they will withdraw and need security because they still have many fears.

4. Emphasize God's love and care for them. Assure the children of your love for them and praise them for their accomplishments.

5. These children may resist personal demands, so teach them obedience.

6. They can sympathize with others; thus, missionary stories make a great impression on them.

D. Socially

1. They will talk with each other and share new items (e.g. what their families will do on vacation). Therefore, encourage them to invite their friends.
2. They are more aware of their own peers than the preschoolers are, but they still enjoy talking to adults. So take time to talk to them about their interests.
3. They like non-competitive group activities, and they want to play with other children, both boys and girls; these classes do not need to be divided by sex.
4. During a recreation time, provide team games for the children.
5. They will enjoy the group activities used for memorizing Scripture.
6. Since they are inclined to be selfish, encourage them to pray for others and help those in need.
7. These children respect authority and want to be grown-up. Therefore, set a good example for them to follow and encourage them to pray for their parents, pastor and teachers.

E. Spiritually

1. These children can have a genuine interest in spiritual things.
2. They like to sing, say their memory verses, hear the Bible lessons and pray.
3. Cultivate this interest by encouraging them to tell others about Christ.
4. Their concept of God is that He is a great individual who created all things.

5. They feel a personal relationship to God, which is displayed in their prayers.

6. Provide opportunities for the children to pray. However, don't coax those who do not wish to pray. Be patient; in time they also will do it.

7. These children want to be good.

8. They should know that God knows all about them and expects them to be good but that being good does not get them to Heaven; Jesus is the only way to get to heaven.

9. Many are ready to accept Jesus as their Savior. Provide opportunity for this in your class time.

10. When you work with these children and observe their enthusiasm for spiritual things, you will realize this is an ideal time to present the gospel and to give them opportunity for response.

LEARNING EXERCISE #3

INSTRUCTIONS: Fill in the blanks from the section you have just read.

1. First through third grade children seem much _____ and _____ than preschool children and there are a few toothless smiles scattered throughout the group.

2. These children love to _____ hard and to _____ hard.

3. In the classroom the children can participate by _____ Scripture, by _____ and _____ in their workbook and by making _____ projects.

4. They are learning to _____ and _____ and they are eager to exercise these newly acquired abilities.

5. These children have good _____, so emphasize Scripture memorization.

6. First through third graders like to play games that use _____ and _____ so they will enjoy the hidden messages in puzzles.

7. They are beginning to _____ and to form some of their own _____.

8. Avoid _____ in your songs and your teaching.

9. These children are _____ and easily excited.

10. They may resist personal demands, so teach them _____.

11. They will _____ with each other and share new items.

12. Since they are inclined to be _____, encourage them to _____ for others and help those in need.

13. They can have a genuine interest in _____.

14. They want to be _____.

V. Fourth, Fifth, and Sixth Grades - 9, 10, and 11-Year-Olds (Jr. Department)

A. Physically

1. Most Juniors are strong, healthy, active students who are full of energy.
2. The girls are beginning to shoot past the boys in height.
3. Juniors usually like being outdoors, which means you may want to have some activities outdoors when the weather permits.
4. Juniors are sometimes noisy and may push and shove occasionally.

5. Allow them some freedom, but only in the right places and at the right times.

B. Mentally

1. Many juniors are mentally sharp.
2. They are probably one year ahead of juniors ten years ago in terms of knowledge and awareness.
3. Juniors love to read and write. Be aware, however, that some may be totally lost in reading the Bible. Never embarrass a junior by asking them to read a verse if they are unable to do so.
4. Juniors are beginning to learn about history and geography.
5. Thinking and reasoning abilities are growing in the junior years.
6. Do not be afraid to ask the students thought questions or ways to apply the lesson to their lives.
7. Because they have good memories, emphasize Scripture memorization.
8. These are searching years for juniors. They are asking questions about life. Give them solid biblical answers.
9. Challenge them with serious thinking.

C. Socially

1. The social aspects of juniors' lives are very important. They need to feel accepted by their peers, which may lead to giving in to peer pressure to be accepted.
2. You will often see juniors forming little groups among themselves. This is not bad as long as it does not turn to cliques.
3. If one student seems to be left out, take extra measures to include him.
4. Junior boys and girls do not like being near each other. You will notice that the boys and girls will usually sit in separate places while in class.

5. Behavioral problems may occur because juniors are sitting next to good friends.

6. While you must demand right behavior, work on earning their respect and attention by your love, concern and interesting and challenging lessons.

7. Juniors are prone to follow someone, either someone in the class or a well-known personality. While this can be healthy, it often is not. Turn their attention to biblical characters and especially the Lord Jesus.

8. Resistance to authority also characterizes juniors. Be firm and yet loving in your classroom control. By submitting to your authority they will learn principles to help them submit to God's authority.

9. Juniors are ready to accept responsibility. Allow the students to do things on their own, but hold them accountable for all their actions.

D. Emotionally

1. Though many of the fears of earlier childhood days are gone, some fears still remain. Juniors will often try to cover them up with the "macho" or "sophisticated" attitude, but do not be deceived. They still need gentle, compassionate care.

2. Many juniors, especially boys, do not like outward displays of affection, so find other means of showing your love and concern.

3. Juniors may also be quick tempered. Try to avoid problem situations and diffuse and potentially explosive situations. Self-control must be taught.

4. Juniors love to laugh and have a good time. However, never let this get out of hand or be at the expense of someone else. Laughter can be cruel and demolishing to a student who is the brunt of a joke.

E. Spiritually

1. The spirit of this age says that spiritual things are not for 'real' men and women. Help juniors to see that this

is not true. In fact, only 'real' men and women care about spiritual things.

2. Most juniors are ready to accept Christ as Savior. Therefore, stress the claims of Christ.

3. Give a salvation invitation in every class.

4. Talk to each student personally about his relationship to the Lord.

5. Juniors can be involved in deep sin. Help them to see that there is victory only in Jesus.

6. These students may have many questions about spiritual matters, and they will not always ask them in class. Spend personal time with them to allow them to open up to you.

7. The Bible is too often a closed book for juniors. Show them that the Bible is relevant to them, and encourage them to have daily devotions.

8. Challenge the juniors to live for the Lord.

9. Be forthright and clear.

10. Apply each Bible lesson to their lives in specific ways.

11. Show them that the way of the Lord is the way of happiness and joy in their lives.

12. Juniors are making decisions that will effect their entire lives. Urge them to look to Christ now and follow Him throughout the rest of their lives.

LEARNING EXERCISE #4

INSTRUCTIONS: Fill in the blanks from the section you have just read.

1. Most Juniors are _____ , _____ , _____ students who are full of _____ .

2. The girls are beginning to shoot past the boys in _____ .

3. Juniors usually like being _____ .
4. Juniors are sometimes noisy and may _____ and _____ occasionally.
5. Many juniors are mentally _____ .
6. Juniors love to _____ and _____ .
7. Juniors are beginning to learn about _____ and _____ .
8. _____ and _____ abilities are growing in the junior years.
9. Juniors need to feel accepted by their peers, which may lead to giving in to peer pressure to be _____ .
10. _____ problems may occur because juniors are sitting next to good friends.
11. Juniors are prone to _____ someone.
12. _____ to authority also characterizes juniors.
13. Juniors are ready to accept _____ .
14. Juniors will often try to cover up their fears with the "_____" or "_____" attitude, but do not be deceived.
15. Juniors may also be _____ - _____ .
16. Juniors love to laugh and have a _____ .
17. Most juniors are ready to _____ Christ as Savior.
18. Juniors can be involved in deep _____ .
19. Challenge the juniors to live for the _____ .

VI. Teens

    A. Physically

        1. Teenagers are concerned about their height, weight, hair styles and other appearance issues.

        2. Puberty often causes growth or development spurts that could result in an unfair comparison with other teens who either have or have not grown. This fact, coupled with the pressure from ads, commercials and other media sources to look like models, can cause extreme anxiety.

        3. Be sympathetic to this pressure and help teens cope with it.

        4. Understand that they may have self-image problems.

        5. Communicate with the group what the appropriate dress will be.

        6. Limit your programming ideas to recreation and classroom activities that will not promote additional anxiety.

    B. Mentally

        1. Teens are often unconcerned about lengthy biblical history or even the future. They want to know how the Bible relates to their lives today.

        2. Be aware of their current needs and teach to meet those needs.

        3. Teens will respond to God's Word if it relates to them personally.

        4. A youth worker needs to be a great motivator. Teens today have too many other attractions to be excited about last decade's motivational techniques.

        5. Keep the meetings alive and moving.

        6. Change teaching methods often.

How To Relate To Your Students

C. **Socially**

1. Peer relationships are quite important and extremely influential in the lives of your teens.
2. Because of this influence, teenagers will seek to be accepted by their peer group.
3. You need to recognize this characteristic and plan your program accordingly.

D. **Emotionally**

1. Never embarrass teenagers because their emotional makeup is fragile.
2. Do not put them "on the spot."
3. Ask for volunteers and prepare them adequately for discussion or question and answer teaching methods.

E. **Spiritual**

1. Current statistics say that 85 percent of those who do not accept Christ by the age of 18 probably never will.
2. Children go to church because their parents do or because some other influential adult does, but teenagers often are given a choice.
3. The teenage years can be a key time for making spiritual decisions and commitments.
4. Stress personal salvation and dedication to Jesus Christ.
5. Many people point back to decisions made for Christ during their teenage years.

LEARNING EXERCISE #5

INSTRUCTIONS: Fill in the blanks from the section you have just read.

1. Teenagers are concerned about their _____ , _____ , _____ styles and other appearance issues.

2. Puberty often causes growth or development spurts that could result in an unfair comparison with other teens who either have or have not _____.

3. Puberty and the pressure from ads, commercials and other media sources to look like models, can cause extreme _____.

4. Understand that they may have _____-_____ problems.

5. Teens are often unconcerned about lengthy biblical _____ or even the _____.

6. Teens want to know how the Bible relates to their lives _____.

7. The teacher should be aware of their current _____ and teach to meet those _____.

8. A youth worker needs to be a great _____.

9. Keep the meetings _____ and _____.

10. Change teaching methods _____.

11. _____ relationships are quite important and extremely influential in the lives of your teens.

12. Never _____ teenagers because their emotional makeup is fragile.

13. Do not put them "_____."

14. Ask for _____ and prepare them adequately for discussion or questions and answer teaching methods.

15. Current statistics say that _____ percent of those who do not accept Christ by the age of _____ probably never will.

16. The teenage years can be a key time for making
    _____ _____ .

VII. Young Adults
A. Physically

1. Young adults are at their prime physically. To have an effective ministry to young adults you must provide activities. The young adult ministries that are growing are the ones with an active program.

2. The teacher of young adults must be a positive, fun, exciting, well-studied motivator and leader. Young adults are looking for someone to follow. They need someone who will make Bible study exciting.

3. The young adult has a high energy level. If this energy is not channeled into spiritual activities, then they will find other areas of activity.

B. Mentally

1. Young adults are either completing their education or are continuing it.

2. Young adults are skeptical. They grow weary of form without function, and of piety and dogma without relevance and power in life.

3. There has always been a natural gap between generations in the sense of tension between adolescents and adults. They are very reluctant to join the adult world' institutions or adopt its customs. They do, however, join groups and movements of their own making or persuasion.

4. This is why it is so important to get them to make their Sunday School class their own.

C. Socially

1. Young adults are confronted with a number of new relationships and responsibilities:
    a. Selecting a mate

b. Learning to live with a marriage partner

c. Starting a family

d. Rearing children

e. Managing a home

f. Getting started in an occupation

g. Taking on civic responsibility

h. Finding a congenial social group

2. These tasks constitute major expectations of society for this age group, but not all young adults work at these in the same way. Some will be hard at work in the beginning stages of these tasks in adolescence. Developing a philosophy of life, viewed as an adolescent task, may be a continuing matter of concern for some young adults.

3. While not all young adults will develop associations with members of the opposite sex that lead to marriage, these expectations of society form a significant part of their thoughts and activities.

D. Emotionally

1. Young adults are searching. The quest is for self. They ask, what kind of person am I? What kind of person ought I to be?

2. The quest of young adults is for others. They want to make friends and be where friends can be made.

3. The quest of young adults is for the meaning in life. They need to be directed to spiritual truths.

E. Spiritually

1. Young adults have great spiritual needs. The cords that bound them to home, school, church and customs have been loosened. The taboos of home and

church are questioned. They find it easy to drop out of spiritual activities.

2. To reach young adults you must first win their attention by ministering to them. This means that young adults must not be expected to serve the church. Instead the church must become aware that young adults have needs of their own which must be served by the church before they are ready to become workers in the church.

3. Young adults must be constantly invited to receive Christ as their Savior, but not pushed.

4. Young adults need to be challenged to give their life to the Lord for full time service. Many adults have lamented the fact that they did not surrender to the Lord sooner. The young adult that surrenders to the Lord's service has their whole life to give for His service.

LEARNING EXERCISE #6

INSTRUCTIONS: Fill in the blanks from the section you have just read.

1. To have an effective ministry to young adults you must provide _____.

2. The teacher of young adults must be a _____, _____, _____, _____, _____ and _____.

3. Young adults are looking for someone to _____.

4. Young adults are either completing their _____ or are continuing it.

5. List eight of the relationships and responsibilities young adults are confronted with:

   a. _____

   b. _____

c. _____

d. _____

e. _____

f. _____

g. _____

h. _____

6. List three things young adults are searching for:

    a. _____

    b. _____

    c. _____

7. To reach young adults you must first win their attention by _____ .

8. Young adults need to be challenged to give their life to the Lord for full time _____ .

VII. Middle Adults

A. Physically

1. Quite often the changes in the biological or physical realm cause the greatest amount of concern to the individual entering middle age. These changes are inescapable. The body experiences less strength and energy, and there is a waning of sexual power and ability. The manner of aging varies as much as individuals do, and much of aging is psychological as well as physical.

2. Middle adults have a tendency to gain weight, to acquire the "middle-age spread," and to gain a receding

hairline or graying hair. Also the texture of the skin tends to grow coarser and wrinkles appear.

3. In the latter part of middle age, the physical senses decline in acuity. Vision can become impaired, hearing may be affected, and even touch and taste can diminish in intensity.

4. This group of adults is more prone to illnesses and diseases than earlier adults.

5. Many adults in their fifties and sixties have been hospitalized for surgery or illnesses common to that age group.

6. Many men who feel the drain of their strength, go to extremes to maintain or assure themselves that they are still physically capable of accomplishing what younger men can do. This in turn can cause serious injury if done in excess, for the motor skills and powers are now less adept.

7. Women, too, tend to spend more time grooming themselves in order to escape the oncoming changes in physical appearance.

B. Mentally

1. Stereotypes abound when the learning ability of middle-age adults is discussed.

2. The belief of severe mental decline and lessening of learning ability is rooted in fables and myths, which unfortunately are taken seriously by some.

3. Studies indicate that after the early twenties, adults experience a small decline in learning or intellectual speed, but this varies considerably from one individual to another. The decline is so gradual that one may not even notice a change.

4. Later research has shown even more positive results in the ability of adults to learn. It may take an older person longer to learn, but the learning capacity remains.

5. Many adults who have been out of a learning context for years and are either unaccustomed to the academic type of learning structure or are out of practice, still rise to the challenge to learn.

C. **Socially**

1. In the social realm a variety of changes occur in middle adulthood. Within family life itself there are adjustments. With the children leaving home and establishing their own families, the home may seem empty, and some couples must learn to adjust to one another.

2. Loneliness may set in and the companionship of the other mate may seem insufficient to compensate for the loss. The difference in the time of the physical change process of men and women may cause strain between them.

3. The prospect of becoming grandparents requires adjustment.

4. For many middle adults, their aging parents present another problem.

5. The middle-aged adult now begins to prefer quieter events such as reading and parties, in comparison to strenuous sports or picnics.

D. **Emotionally**

1. Studies of social participation have shown that membership in formal community, church and business groups is low during early adulthood but reaches a peak in the late forties or early fifties before it begins to decline.

2. Middle-age is the time for service. More time can now be given to church work.

3. The middle adult's emotional outlook on his physical changes is just as important as the biological changes themselves. As aging continues, it is easy to slide

into a process of deterioration, especially with the loss of sensory props. How the person has viewed and prepared for this stage of life is involved in the reaction that occurs.

4. Insecurity can arise, depression is common (especially with women and their physical change), and self-abasement may occur as uselessness (whether real or imagined) is felt.

5. In teaching middle adults, certain characteristics of their learning state must be considered:

   a. Many of these adults do not come to a learning environment with a learner's attitude. For most of the week they are involved in producing, but now they sit and absorb.

   b. They have more definite and concrete ideas than others, even to the extent of rigidity.

   c. They come with a backlog of experiences from life, which enables them to contribute more to a learning experience and to assimilate new information and experiences more effectively and readily.

   d. They are used to an immediate application of information. They want to know, *"How is this relevant to my life right now?"*

E. Spiritually

1. In sheer numbers the middle-aged comprise the bulk of the membership in many if not most local churches.

2. They are also the church's backbone in leadership, experiences, and potentialities.

3. For these reasons and because the range of interests and needs of middle adults is so wide, the church's educational program for this age group is highly significant.

4. The following general suggestions are given as basic guidelines for a church educational ministry to middle adults, based on their characteristics and needs:
    a. Teach the Bible creatively and relevantly.
    b. Provide instruction and guidance on potential issues of adult life.
    c. Offer instruction and counsel on how middle adults can adjust to difficult circumstances of life.
    d. Encourage adults to plan and participate in adult social and recreational activities.
    e. Evangelize adults through personal witness, visitation, and neighborhood and business associates.

LEARNING EXERCISE #7

INSTRUCTIONS: Fill in the blanks from the section you have just read.

1. Quite often the changes in the _____ or _____ realm cause the greatest amount of concern to the individual entering middle age.

2. In the latter part of middle age the physical senses decline in _____.

3. Many men who feel the drain of their strength go to extremes to maintain or assure themselves that they are still _____ capable of accomplishing what younger men can do.

4. Studies indicate that after the early twenties adults experience a _____ decline in learning or intellectual speed, but this varies considerably from one individual to another.

5. Middle age is the time for _____ .

6. The middle adult's emotional outlook on his physical changes is just as important as the _____ themselves.

7. Many middle adults do not come to a learning environment with a learner's _____ .

8. List four basic guidelines for a church educational ministry to middle adults:

    a. _____

    b. _____

    c. _____

    d. _____

VIII. Senior Adults

A. Physically

1. Senior adults' physical health and vigor gradually declines.

2. They may suddenly be hit with an illness or have an accident which will leave them in a semi-invalid condition for years before their death.

3. The decline in church attendance is often due to physical problems. Some of these hindering conditions are as obvious as the problems of stairs to climb, slippery floors to navigate, restrooms inaccessible to the disabled, poor acoustics that confuse the hard-of-hearing or produce a thunderous roar in their hearing aids, and drafty air circulation.

4. Others have a problem of transportation. They no longer drive or no longer drive at night.

B. Mentally

1. There is a self-defeating attitude among senior adults, that *"you can't teach an old dog new tricks."*

2. Many aging persons will refuse to study, memorize scripture and engage in other educational activities.

3. They have forgotten that people are not dogs, and they fail to realize that learning is practiced continually as they

adjust to new circumstances of their own lives and to changes in society.

C. Socially

1. The coming of Social Security, Medicare, and other governmental provisions for some of the needs of the aging has produced important changes in their status. Now most of their material needs can be met, even if poorly, without direct dependence on children or other younger relatives. This has reduced the potentiality for and the reality of many interpersonal stresses and has also made it less likely that they will live in the same household as younger generations. Social isolation is common among the elderly as a result, yet it may not be as widespread as many people think.

2. New patterns of housing for older adults have contributed to a sense of 'loneliness in the crowd' for many. These patterns include retirement communities and mobile home parks.

3. Strained marital relationships may result from the retirement of a husband who suddenly is around home all the time 'interfering' with what has previously been the wife's exclusive daytime domain.

D. Emotionally

1. Emotional and mental problems are common, and many spiritual problems emerge as well.

    a. For instance, they may experience a subtle sense of guilt sensed for departure from moral standards they were taught in childhood as they conform to changes in society around them.

    b. They may have fears of the future because of uncertainties about the forgiveness of sins or other aspects of their relationship to God.

    c. When to these are added the physical and social barriers placed in the way of their participation in church life, the burden of many seem nearly insurmountable.

2. A bleak, pessimistic spirit is common among the aged. It is present to a greater degree among those who are in poor health, persons of lower socioeconomic status, those who reside in rural areas, and those who are retired, in contrast to their counterpart categories, and it is more common among men than among women.

E. **Spiritually**

1. Church attendance tends to decline during the later years of old age in typical congregations, so some have concluded that people become less spiritual near the conclusion of life. They have failed to consider other indicators of spiritual behavior, including prayer and Bible reading. On the basis of these and other criteria it can be said that in general there is an increase in religious commitment with advancing age.

2. One third of the total membership of many church congregations is past the age of sixty-five.

3. Many a non-Christian begins to give serious thought to religion and life beyond the grave only when he is retired and relieved of the pressures of other responsibilities that earlier choked the word that was sown so that it could not bear fruit.

4. When Christians fail to seek them out through friendship and love in their hour of need, they become the victims of cults established by leaders eager to profit from their unease.

5. Research perhaps would reveal four main reasons for the failure of senior adult church members to attend:

    a. Some find the curriculum and teaching irrelevant to their current needs.

    b. Others find them to be repetitious of what they have 'always had' in lessons during previous stages of the life cycle.

    c. Some face complications of physical health, problems of transportation, or difficulties in sitting through two hours of activities.

    d. Some have either drifted from their faith or never truly possessed it.

LEARNING EXERCISE #8

INSTRUCTIONS: Fill in the blanks from the section you have just read.

1. Senior adult's physical health and vigor gradually _____ .

2. The decline in church attendance is often due to _____ .

3. Many aging persons will refuse to study, memorize scripture and engage in other _____ activities.

4. _____ isolation is common among the elderly.

5. Strained _____ may result from the retirement of a husband, who suddenly is around home all the time 'interfering' with what has previously been the wife's exclusive daytime domain.

6. A bleak, pessimistic spirit is common among the _____ .

7. _____ - _____ of the total membership of many church congregations is past the age of sixty-five.

8. List four main reasons for the failure of senior adult church members to attend:
   a. _____
   b. _____
   c. _____
   d. _____

X. Single Adults

A. Unmarried adults

1. The social and theological attitude which confronts the unmarried are closely related.

2. Satisfactory fulfillment of adult social roles is primarily defined in terms of marriage and family relationships, thus the unmarried is atypical socially in terms of the larger social order.

3. While our society has a general attitude of acceptance towards unmarrieds, they are, nevertheless, put under a heavy social disadvantage.

4. Unless the church is able to overcome this failure, it will not likely have to bother with other problems mentioned below, for it will have pushed its unmarried adults out into the subculture of the unmarried to find subgroup acceptance instead of self-acceptance and God-acceptance.

5. Three problems related to the unmarried must be dealt with realistically by the church:

    a. aloneness

    b. loneliness

    c. sexuality

6. Aloneness and loneliness are not the same but may grow out of each other. The 'family church' with its emphasis on family programs may inadvertently isolate the unmarried. Aloneness may turn to an emotional dejection which results in personal isolation. If this happens the unmarried persons may then turn to groups outside the church to find companionship and meaning for their type of life.

B. Divorced

1. Of the many problems the church faces in ministering to the divorced, perhaps none is more important than the attitude it communicates about divorce. Unless there is enough grace flowing from Christ, through His church, so that the divorced person can sense the potential of reconciliation and fellowship within the church, he will probably turn to other agencies for help with problems stemming from his divorced status.

2. The problems related to divorce are often complex, requiring resources and professional skills beyond the resources of a particular church. For this reason some churches have found their most useful role to be a supportive one, supporting the family in its spiritual growth while cooperating with social agencies that deal with financial and social matters.

C. Widowed

1. The widow has been a special concern of the church through all ages, and specific biblical teachings of the care of the widowed have offered suggestions and stated responsibilities toward them.

2. The plight of the widow is often used in Scripture to emphasize trust in and dedication to God, and to prick the conscience of the socially irresponsible. (See Mark 12:42; Luke 4:26; 18:3 5; 1 Timothy 5:3 16; James 1:27).

3. From a theological viewpoint, the church plays a vital role in providing the sympathy, understanding and love needed during bereavement.

4. While the church cannot take the place of the lost mate, people within it can assume other social roles that make it possible for the widowed to establish new social relationships.

5. This is a big step in helping a person maintain his desire for life, to develop new goals, and to find fruitful use of his time.

6. Some churches have found widowed people ready to take on more active roles in Christian service, such as visitation, administrative responsibilities, etc.

LEARNING EXERCISE #9

INSTRUCTIONS: Fill in the blanks from the section you have just read.

1. While our _____ society has a general attitude of acceptance toward the unmarried, they are, nevertheless, put under a heavy disadvantage.

2. What are the three problems related to the unmarried?

   a. _____

   b. _____

   c. _____

3. Of the many problems the church faces in ministering to the divorced, perhaps none is more important than the _____ it communicates about divorce.

4. The problems related to divorce are often complex, requiring resources and professional skills beyond the resources of a particular.

5. From a theological viewpoint, the church can play a vital role in providing the _____ , _____ and _____ needed during bereavement.

CHAPTER REVIEW (For *Certificate of Completion*)

INSTRUCTIONS: Write the group in the blank that the sentence best describes: 2 & 3 year-olds; 4 & 5 year-olds; 6, 7 & 8 year-olds; 9, 10 & 11 year-olds; Teens; Young Adults; Middle Adult; Senior Adult; Widowed; Unmarried; Divorced.

1. _____ They are inquisitive, have a short attention span, believe their teacher, and do not understand symbolism.

2. _____ They are strong, healthy, active students who are full of energy.

3. _____ Their physical health and vigor gradually declines.

4. _____ They are concerned about their height, weight, hair styles and other appearance issues.

5. _____ They enjoy acting out a Bible story.

6. _____ There are three problems (aloneness, loneliness, sexuality) related to this group.

7. _____ In the classroom they can participate by memorizing Scripture, by writing and coloring in their workbook and by making craft projects.

8. _____ To have an effective ministry to this group you must provide activities.

9. _____ Quite often the changes in the biological or physical realm cause the greatest amount of concern to the individuals entering this group.

10. _____ Of the many problems the church faces in ministering to this group perhaps none is more important than the attitude it communicates.

11. _____ They are dependent, self-centered, play alone, like friends and need attention.

12. _____ A bleak, pessimistic spirit is common among this group.

13. _____ They are sometimes noisy and may push and shove occasionally.

14. _____ Never embarrass them because their emotional makeup is fragile.

15. _____ Their attention span is increasing. They love to ask questions. Their vocabulary is increasing. They like to use their imagination.

16. _____ They do not come to a learning environment with a learner's attitude.

17. _____ They are impatient and easily excited.

18. _____ The teacher of this group must be positive, fun, exciting, well studied motivator and leader.

19. _____ From a theological viewpoint, the church can play a vital role in providing the sympathy, understanding and love needed by this group.

20. _____ He wants to pray, is interested in the Bible, wants to know about God, and senses the wonders of God.

21. _____ He thinks of God in a personal way, understands the difference between right and wrong, and can understand the Bible is God's special Book.

22. _____ Peer relationships are quite important and extremely influential in their lives.

23. _____ One third of the total membership of many church congregations is made up of this group.

24. _____ This age group is a time for service.

25. _____ They will often try to cover up their fears with the 'macho' or 'sophisticated' attitude.

CHAPTER NINE
HOW TO SCHEDULE YOUR TIME

I. INTRODUCTION

When I was a teenager I took numerous canoe trips on rivers in Michigan. Most of the rivers I canoed on were not particularly hazardous so a guide was not needed. With a reliable outfitter, good maps, and some wilderness proficiency, most canoeists could handle the experience by themselves.

There are other areas of the world, however, such as the Himalayas, where having a seasoned guide is a matter of life and death. Imagine we're exploring that dangerous area and our guide, whom we've never met before, comes out to greet us. After exchanging initial pleasantries, he begins to speak of the region we're about to visit. Our guide tells us he's never been there before but assures us it's beautiful. "Oh, yes," he mentions, "it's true, we'll encounter some potentially dangerous situations, but I don't think we'll experience any real problems at least I hope not; after all, I don't have a first aid kit."

By the time this alleged guide asks if anyone in our group has a map and compass he can borrow, the picture has become very clear. This man is not qualified to be a member of our group, let alone guide us. Needless to say, our plans change on the spot. If we still want to explore the area, we will hire a trained guide. No group wants a leader who is inexperienced, unskilled, and unprepared.

In many ways, a Sunday School teacher is similar to a guide. A guide must be well acquainted with the area a group's planning to explore before he can help others discover it.

A good Sunday School teacher will have his class planned out. The following schedule is a good pattern to follow.

II. Sunday Morning Schedule
A. Before Sunday School
1. The teacher should get up early enough so as to avoid any rushing.

2. The teacher should brush over his lesson for the task at hand.
3. He should dress himself properly so as to be a good example.
4. He should arrive fifteen minutes early to prepare the classroom for the lesson.
5. He should then stand at the door to greet the class members as they enter.
6. The teacher should properly meet and greet all visitors before the beginning of the opening assembly.

B. Opening Assembly

1. This opening assembly should begin with pledges to the American flag, Christian flag and the Bible.
2. Then the superintendent should lead in prayer.
3. After prayer it's good to have a good rousing chorus or hymn.
4. We have found it is best to receive the Sunday School offering during this opening assembly rather than in the individual classes.
5. This opening assembly should include adequate welcoming of visitors.
6. The superintendent should certainly promote attendance for future Sundays, give honor to those who have done good jobs in the past, recognize birthdays and anniversaries, and instill and inspire in the hearts of the pupils the desire to bring others with them.
7. The entire opening exercise should last no longer than ten minutes. For a Sunday School that lasts one hour, this gives ten minutes for time spent in going to the class and in business.

C. Class time

1. The teacher welcomes each student

      a. After dismissal to their Sunday School classes the teachers should once again personally greet each student. Shake their hand, look them in the eye and call them by their name.

      b. Visitors may be introduced by the teacher or someone else in the class (person who invited them). But, whoever does it should be effervescent. In smaller classes all the members of the class should then be introduced or introduce themselves to him.

2. Refreshment time provides an opportunity for the teacher of children to talk with each of the students and get to know them better. For the adults it gives a time of fellowship and an opportunity to bond with one another.

3. Class business should be limited basically to the announcements and taking roll. All planning of socials and extracurricular activities should be done prior to class time and business cared for in class should be limited to announcements, and simple promotion, etc.

4. Every Sunday School class should have a prayer list.

      a. All prayer requests should be placed on this list.

      b. Keep the list up to date.

      c. Include all the students in the class as well as new prospects on the list.

      d. Encourage your class to pray for the names on the list every day.

      e. The teacher can ask if someone would like to lead in prayer, but never call on someone without checking with them prior to class.

D. Review

1. In children's departments, reviews may take the forms of games.

2. In teen and adult departments, they may still take that form. As such, they will be remembered longer because of the unique approach.

3. Occasional tests may be given younger students, perhaps as a printed summary of the previous lesson, with two or three incorrect statements or words omitted to be corrected and/or identified.

4. Remember, teaching builds on former lessons, and new lessons must be integrated in the total experience of the pupil. A new lesson is not a continuation of last week's lesson, but it should remind the student what was communicated in the previous lesson.

E. **Teaching of lesson**

1. Teachers must begin the lesson where pupils are and take them where they should go.

2. An introduction is imperative in teaching.

3. Since teaching is the guidance of learning activities, guides must make contact with their followers before they begin to guide.

4. Do not start the class by announcing, *"I'm starting"* or *"Come to order."* This method will soon lose its effectiveness and become non-productive.

F. **Invitation**

a. The invitation can be given by a raise of hands with heads bowed.

b. Another approach is to have students who wish to make a decision to remain seated after the class is dismissed.

c. The best method is to visit the student in their home.

d. Never put a student on the spot before the class! You can embarrass them to the point where they will never come back and may never make a decision.

G. **Closing Prayer** - Again, pray for the special requests that were made that day and any decisions that were made in class during invitation.

H. **Memory Work** - This is mostly a children's activity. Adults like to learn Scripture, but usually not in groups and not by childish methods. On the other hand, children love memory work. It is the way the Bible is carried home in their hearts.

I. **Work Sheets**
1. Most children's lessons and teen's lessons have a work sheet at the end of the lesson that is to be completed.
2. The worksheets will vary: a picture to be colored; a craft to be constructed; or a puzzle to be completed, etc.

J. **Clean Up**
1. Teachers are responsible for their class cleanup.
2. They should not dismiss their class until the entire area has been straightened up.

LEARNING EXERCISE #1

INSTRUCTIONS: Fill in the blanks from the section you have just read.

1. A good Sunday School teacher will have their class _____.

2. The Sunday School teacher should arrive _____ minutes early to prepare the classroom for the lesson.

3. The teacher should properly meet and greet all _____ before the starting of the opening assembly.

4. The entire opening exercise should last no longer than _____ minutes.

5. After dismissal to their Sunday School classes the teacher should once again personally _____ each student.

6. Refreshment time for the adults gives a time of _____ and an opportunity to _____ with one another.

7. Class business should be limited basically to the _____ and _____ .

8. Every Sunday School class should have a _____.

9. The teacher can ask if someone would like to lead in prayer, but should not call on someone without checking with them prior to class.

10. Remember, teaching builds on _____ lessons, and new lessons must be _____ in the total experience of the pupil.

11. Teachers must begin the lesson where the pupils _____ and _____ them where they should go.

12. Do not start the class by announcing, "_____": or "_____."

13. The invitation can be given by a _____ with heads bowed.

14. Never put a student on the _____ before the class.

15. You can embarrass a student to the point where they will never come back and may never make a _____ .

16. Teachers are responsible for their class _____-_____ .

CHAPTER REVIEW (For *Certificate of Completion*)

INSTRUCTIONS: Write 'T' if the sentence is true, 'F' if the sentence is false.

1. _____ Never put a student on the spot before the class.
2. _____ Teachers must begin the lesson where the pupils are and take them where they should go.

How To Schedule Your Time

3. _____ A good Sunday School teacher will have their class planned out.

4. _____ The entire opening exercise should last no longer than thirty minutes.

5. _____ Class business should be limited basically to the announcements and taking roll.

6. _____ The Sunday School teacher should arrive one minute early to prepare the classroom for the lesson. Do not start the class by announcing "I'm starting" or "come to order."

7. _____ Refreshment time for the adults gives a time of fellowship and an opportunity to bond with one another.

8. _____ Teaching builds on former lessons, and new lessons must be integrated in the total experience of the pupil.

9. _____ The teacher should properly meet and greet all visitors before the starting of the opening assembly.

10. _____ Every Sunday School class should have a prayer list.

11. _____ Teachers should call on all the members of the class to pray at least once.

12. _____ Teachers are responsible for their class cleanup.

13. _____ The invitation can be given by a raise of hands with heads bowed.

14. _____ After dismissal to their Sunday School classes the teacher should once again personally greet each student.

CHAPTER TEN
DISCIPLINE - HOW TO KEEP CONTROL OF YOUR CLASS

I. Introduction

There was a boy in our church a few years ago who was always fighting. If he didn't get his way, or if a teacher tried to correct him, he would throw a temper tantrum. At every teacher's meeting the same topic would come up, *"What are we going to do with this child?"*

We spoke with the parents and they blamed the boy's fighting and undisciplined behavior on the other students and the teacher's inability to teach. They said he was a good boy and had no problem.

They left our church and went to another church thinking that would solve the problem. Not long after they had joined the other church one of the church staff came to me and asked about this boy. They said he was disrupting his Sunday School class, his Awana club, and the Children's Choir. They said they didn't know what to do with him.

The tremendous discipline problems encountered today in a growing work for God cannot be compared to simple problems of the past. Some would say, "It is just too much to take. Let us just call off our efforts to reach them." The result of this attitude is finalized in multitudes going to hell when they could have been reached. We must never give up! We must realize the value of precious souls and the ability of God to change lives.

God is the author of law and order; Satan is the author of confusion and chaos. The words 'disciple' and 'discipline' come from a word that means 'trained in orderliness.' For this reason Christians are admonished: *"Let all things be done decently and in order"* (I Corinthians 14:40).

The Bible also teaches that children are to be brought up in the nurture and admonition of the Lord (Ephesians 6:4). Nurture is instruction, admonition is discipline. Teachers and leaders must not only instruct, but also exercise discipline. Students should learn to think. Moral and spiritual development requires that they also be trained in orderliness.

Disorder interferes with learning. Effective teaching is impossible when a class is out of control. Disorderly students interfere with the teacher's efforts. Instead of practicing obedience, reverence, and the principles of Christian conduct, they learn disrespect for teachers and disregard for God's Word.

Good discipline does not just happen. It results from specific preparation on your part. The following sections will help you reduce and deal with discipline problems.

II. Why do children misbehave?

In order to use correct discipline we must understand the root of the problem. It is not enough just to treat the symptoms.

1. Human beings are sinners by nature. The Word of God is clear in stating we are born in sin. We are sinners by conception, by choice, and by conduct.

2. Satan is against the work of God. Any way you look at it, if we are doing a work for God, Satan will fight it. He has won the victory when we develop a defeated attitude and give up.

3. Bad home situations

4. It is impossible to adequately describe the pitiful conditions of most homes in America.

5. Teachers should visit the homes of pupils.

6. This enables them to understand more fully the problems they face.

A. Physical disabilities

1. One teacher was guilty of correcting a child for talking too loud in the class. Later she discovered the child was deaf and did not realize the loudness of his voice.

2. Many poor children come to Sunday School fatigued. They have had very little rest because of fighting in the home during the night.
3. Many have poor vision, retardation, hearing problems, and sickness.

B. No instruction on proper behavior

1. We must realize that many who come to our churches have never been instructed in proper behavior and must be taught even the simplest rules of courtesy.

C. Permissive public schools

1. In many public schools today the authority is in the students' hands.
2. The teachers and administrators work in fear.
3. The students are actually in control, if those public school officials would ever admit it.
4. When pupils come to the Sunday School with this kind of attitude, problems will soon develop.

D. Fear

1. Many children are afraid.
2. They enter a new room and meet new people.
3. They do not know how they will be treated.
4. They react out of fear.

E. They are starving for love and attention.

1. Many children in America today know nothing of what it means to be loved and cared for.
2. The only way they know how to get attention is to misbehave.

LEARNING EXERCISE #1

INSTRUCTIONS: Fill in the blanks from the section you have just read.

1. The tremendous discipline problems encountered today in a growing work for God cannot be compared to simple problems of the _____ .

2. We must realize the value of precious souls and the ability of God to _____ .

3. God is the author of _____ and _____ .

4. Satan is the author of _____ and _____ .

5. The words "disciple" and "discipline" come from a word that means "_____."

6. The Bible also teaches that children are to be brought up in the _____ and _____ of the Lord.

7. Nurture is _____ ; admonition is _____ .

8. Teachers and leaders must not only instruct, but also exercise _____.

9. _____ interferes with learning.

10. Good discipline does not just _____ .

11. In order to use correct discipline we must understand the _____ of the problem.

12. We are sinners by _____ , by _____ , and by _____ .

13. _____ is against the work of God.

14. Teachers should visit the homes of _____ , to more fully understand the problems he faces.

15. List four disabilities a student may have:

a. _____
b. _____
c. _____
d. _____

16. List eight reasons why children misbehave:

   a. _____
   b. _____
   c. _____
   d. _____
   e. _____
   f. _____
   g. _____
   h. _____

III. Preventive Measures

Your first goal should be to prevent control problems from happening. Here are some suggestions to help in that:

   A. Be organized.
   1. If you have to fumble around for your next point, you have invited disaster.
   2. Being organized helps prevent the students from becoming overly restless.

   B. Involve the students in the lesson. You can do such things as:
   1. Asking the students questions
   2. Letting them act out the stories
   3. Hand out workbooks and supplies

   C. Smile at the students and show love to them.
   1. They will respond better to you if they perceive you as a friend.
   2. Talk to them and give them proper attention.

3. Many behavior problems start because the students want attention and will do whatever is needed to get it.

4. Speak enthusiastically, for this will help the students follow you better.

D. Commend proper behavior with words or actual rewards.

1. This tells the students you are noticing them and that you are pleased with them.

E. Have a set of rules for the class and be sure every student knows them.

1. You may want to have the students themselves choose the rules.

2. Post the rules and the consequences for breaking them so everyone knows what to expect.

3. Be consistent in enforcing the rules.

4. Some examples of rules:

    a. Come in quietly

    b. Sit down

    c. Keep your hands to yourself

    d. When I'm talking, you're not

F. Have a helper in the classroom

1. This person can give greater attention to control matters and may keep you from having to stop the lesson to handle a problem. It is always good to have a man as a helper, because it seems he often conveys more of an authority figure.

LEARNING EXERCISE #2

INSTRUCTIONS: Fill in the blanks from the section you have just read.

1. Your first goal should be to _____ control problems from happening.

2. Being organized helps prevent the students from becoming overly _____ .
3. _____ the students in the lesson.
4. _____ at the students and show _____ to them.
5. Many behavior problems start because the students want _____ and will do whatever is needed to _____ .
6. Commend proper behavior with words or actual _____ .
7. Have a _____ for the class and be sure every student knows them.
8. Have a _____ in the classroom.

IV. Control Measures That Don't Stop the Lesson

Even when you do your best to prevent control problems, they are still going to happen. However, try to handle them, if possible, without stopping class and interrupting the other students. Here are some suggestions for doing this:

A. **Change the pace of the lesson**. Slow it down, speed it up, shout or whisper in order to focus attention on the lesson again.

B. **Look at the students directly** for a few moments or gesture at them while still carrying on the lesson. This will be a signal to them to stop their misbehavior.

C. **Move closer to the students** and maybe even put your hand on their shoulders. This lets the students know that you are aware of what they are doing and that they should stop.

D. **Ask a question** and put the students' name at the end. This will bring their attention back to the lesson and let them know that you are watching them.

E. **Ignore the misbehavior** if possible.

1. Sometimes you must do this if it will not disturb the class too much.
2. Usually what that student wants is attention, and stopping the lesson to focus on him will give him exactly what he wants. He will have won!
3. Ignore his behavior and give him attention in other ways.

LEARNING EXERCISE #3

INSTRUCTIONS: Fill in the blanks from the section you have just read.

1. Even when you do your best to prevent control problems, they are still going to _____ .
2. Try to handle problems, if possible, without stopping class and interrupting the other _____ .
3. Change the _____ of the lesson.
4. _____ at the student directly for a few moments or _____ at him while still carrying on the lesson.
5. Move closer to the student and maybe even put your _____ on his shoulder.
6. Ask a question and put the _____ at the end.
7. Ignore the _____ if possible.

V. Control Measures That Stop the Lesson

Sometimes you must stop the class to handle the problem. You should do this only after you have tried other measures, because stopping the class interrupts all the students. Here are some suggestions for control measures to use when you have to stop the lesson:

A. First, use positive approach.

1. *"I like the way Janie is sitting, listening, watching (whatever), she looks so nice."*
2. *"I'm checking hands and feet or eyes."*

B.   Stop the class and focus attention on that student. Ask him to change whatever he is doing.

C.   Change the seating of the student. Ask the student to sit in a different place or to sit by you.

D.   Speak in a low, firm voice.

E.   If at a table, have him put his head down for a short time. Do not forget about him.

F.   If you notice a teen is talking or misbehaving in class, call him aside after class and talk individually to him.

1. Remind him that you did not embarrass him publicly.
2. Don't use threats.
3. Encourage positive behavior.
4. If a teen continues to disrupt the class, stop teaching for a few moments, look specifically at him and ask for his cooperation.

G.   After all else fails, use a three count.

"That's one," [don't quarrel or argue] "that's two, that's three"

1. They must remain out of class for remainder of the period and next week's class.
2. After Sunday School or church, it is the teacher's responsibility to go to the parents and explain the behavior problem. Be specific.
3. Have the teacher next to you keep an eye on your class if you must take someone out.
4. If the parent is in the church, take the child to the parent.
5. If it is a bus child, take them to their bus captain.
6. Sunday School teachers need to communicate with the Junior Church workers if a child has acquired a one or two count in the Sunday School.
7. Remember, the three count system is to be used only if all else fails.

H. There are some don'ts:
1. Don't snap or shhh or yell.
2. Don't say; *"Who did it?"*
3. Don't wait till you have a big problem nip it in the bud.
   a. Don't wait till everyone is talking, catch the first one.
   b. Don't wait until everyone is out of their seat running around, catch the first one.
   c. Don't wait until everyone is throwing paper wads, catch the first one.
4. Don't be sarcastic.
5. Don't threaten or nag.
6. Don't label children. [*"You're a real dummy, brat, angel, etc."*]
7. Never act exasperated in front of students.
8. NEVER grab, shake, spank, slap, jerk or manhandle a child.
9. All physical contact should be limited, it's best not to touch a child in this day in which we are living.

LEARNING EXERCISE #4

INSTRUCTIONS: Fill in the blanks from the section you have just read.

1. Sometimes you must stop the class to handle the _____ .

2. You should stop the class only after you have tried other measures, because stopping the class _____ all the students.

3. List five control measures that stop the lesson:
   a. _____
   b. _____

c. _____

d. _____

4. If you notice a teen is talking or misbehaving in class, call him aside and talk individually to him.

5. If a teen continues to disrupt the class, stop teaching for a few moments, look specifically at him and _____ .

6. After all else fails, use a _____ .

7. List eight things you should never do:

a. _____

b. _____

c. _____

d. _____

e. _____

f. _____

g. _____

h. _____

CHAPTER REVIEW (For *Certificate of Completion*)

INSTRUCTIONS: Write 'T" if the sentence is true, 'F" if the sentence is false.

1. _____ The tremendous discipline problems encountered today are no different then the problems of the past.

2. _____ God is the author of law and order.

3. _____ Satan is the author of confusion and chaos.

4. _____ Teachers and leaders must not only instruct, but also exercise discipline.

5. _____ Teachers should visit the homes of pupils, to more fully understand the problems he faces.

6. _____ Children who are starving for love may misbehave.

7. _____ Your second goal should be to prevent control problems from happening.

8. _____ Being organized helps prevent the students from becoming overly restless.

9. _____ Teachers should involve the students in the lesson.

10. _____ A teacher should smile at the students and show love to them.

11. _____ Many behavior problems start because the students want attention and will do whatever is needed to get it.

12. _____ Teachers should commend proper behavior with words or actual rewards.

13. _____ Teachers should have a set of rules for the class and be sure every student knows them.

14. _____ When you do your best to prevent control problems, they will not happen.

15. _____ The teacher should try to handle problems, if possible, without stopping the class and interrupting the other students.

16. _____ A teacher should never ignore the misbehavior of a student.

17. _____ Sometimes you must stop the class to handle the problem.

18. _____ You should stop the class only after you have tried other measures, because stopping the class interrupts all the students.

19. _____ Speaking in a low, firm voice will sometimes correct a child.

20. _____ If you notice a teen talking you should embarrass him in front of the other students.

21. _____ After all else fails use the three count.

22. _____ You should never act exasperated in front of students.

23. _____ You should never grab, shake, spank, slap, jerk, or manhandle a child.

CHAPTER ELEVEN
HOW TO BUILD YOUR CLASS

I. Introduction

A preacher told about his seventy year old father who came into his office and said *"Son, I just ordered some fruit trees."*

The preacher leaned back in his chair and chuckled as he thought, *"That old codger is seventy years old and he is out planting fruit trees, it would take between 10 to 15 years to produce fruit."*

He asked his father, *"Who do you think is going to eat the fruit?"*

He said, *"I plan to be around to eat the fruit off the trees that I plant."*

That's the kind of attitude we need to have to keep going, looking to the future with a goal to reach.

When I started Liberty Baptist Church I set a goal of 100 on our first anniversary. On our first anniversary we didn't have 100, we had 163 present, and the building was packed to capacity.

In order to build your Sunday School class you must set goals. The old adage: 'If you aim *at nothing, you are sure to hit it!"* is true in Sunday School work. Without goal-setting there will be no growth.

II. What Is A Goal?

A. A goal is a deliberate, premeditated, intentional aim that we seek to accomplish.

B. A list of synonyms adds words as: intention, end, ambition, and destination.

C. A goal ought not be beyond accomplishment, it ought not be complicated, yet it ought not be too simple.

D. An aim takes awareness of individual needs, and it takes knowledge of the ensuing course.

E. Perhaps, in today's language, the worker might ask himself: "Where am I going today? Where do I want to be next week? Where should I end up at the end of the year?"

III. **Who Should Set Goals?**

   A. Everyone who teaches a Sunday School class should set a goal.

   B. Some teachers may be satisfied with how many students they already have. Their goal should be to build their class to the point where it could be split and become two classes.

   C. Without a goal a Sunday School class will not grow and it will become complacent, stale and stagnant.

   D. If a class is not growing it is dying.

IV. **Why Should Se Set Goals?**

   A. It is easier to make decisions when you know what you are trying to accomplish for the Lord.

   B. Goals are confidence builders, as you set out to achieve those heights that God has laid on your heart.

   C. Goals save time. They make you do what is necessary to do.

   D. Goals that are clearly visualized create a perception so that you are able to see around you the resources that are needed to reach your objectives.

   E. Goals provide a sense of order and purpose and create high interest and motivation over a longer period of time.

   F. Goals with motivation are the wheels that make the world roll, and control the speed at which it rolls.

V. **How Does A Teacher Formulate Goals?**

   A. First, teachers need to set long-term goals.

   1. What do they plan to achieve in the next quarter, in the next year?

   2. They should also set here-and-now goals.

How To Build Your Class

- B. Goals must be written down.
    1. If the goals are not written down then there will not be a real commitment to them.
    2. Commitment is essential for achievement.
    3. Goals not written down are seldom achieved.
- C. Goals must be precise.
    1. Clarity of purpose is the key to getting people excited about a matter.
    2. Wanting to do better is not a clear goal.
    3. A clear goal is that I will visit three hours every week.
- D. Goals must have time limits that are measurable.
    1. You may not accomplish all that you desire to accomplish in a given time frame.
    2. Without time limits you will not be able to measure your success or evaluate problem areas.
- E. Goals must be published, stated openly, shared. Until you do this you do not have goals, but rather you are still at the desired stage.

LEARNING EXERCISE #1

INSTRUCTIONS: Fill in the blanks from the section you have just read.

1. In order to build your Sunday School class you must _____ .

2. What is a goal? _____ _____ _____ .

3. A goal ought not be _____ accomplishment, it ought not be _____ , yet it ought not be _____ .

4. An aim takes _____ and _____, it takes _____ of individual needs, and it takes _____ of the ensuing course.

5. Everyone who teaches a Sunday School class should _____ .

6. Without a goal a Sunday School class will not grow and it will become _____ , _____ , and _____ .

7. It is easier to make _____ when you know what you are trying to accomplish for the Lord.

8. List four reasons for setting goals:
    a. _____
    b. _____
    c. _____
    d. _____
    e. _____

9. A teacher needs first to set _____ - term goals.

10. Goals must be _____ .

11. Goals must be _____ .

12. Goals must have time limits that are _____ .

13. Goals must be _____ , _____ , and _____ .

VI. How Do We Achieve Our Goals?

After setting a goal, an equally difficult task lies in how to accomplish the set goal. An unaccomplished goal is as futile as no goal. Attainment requires a specific goal within reach, along with an explicit plan for arriving there. The following ways can be used to reach your goal:

    A. **Make a poster.**

        1. On the poster write your goal and place it some place where your entire class can see it.

2. Include the date and even a slogan as to how you are going to reach it.

B. Pray every day.

1. God answers the prayers of those who ask for their ministry to be enlarged, but prayer alone cannot build a Sunday School.
2. God will not do what He has commanded us to do.
3. We are to go and reach people. Classes grow when teachers are busy visiting, phoning, mailing, and praying all week.

C. Set a numerical goal.

1. Someone will say, *"All you are interested in is getting numbers."*
2. Well, every number is a precious soul that is going to live as long as God lives in heaven or hell.
3. If they want to criticize us for getting numbers, let them. Praise God! Let us get every number we can.

D. Set a goal for finding new prospects.

1. If your class is going to grow, attempt to get twice as many prospects as your average attendance.
2. This means that each member should suggest two names. If there are seven in the class, get fourteen names on your prospect list.
3. To have a growing Sunday School class, put as much emphasis on finding prospects as on recruiting them.

E. Assign prospect responsibility.

1. Type the names of all prospects on sheets of paper, then distribute copies in the class, assigning prospects to be contacted before the next week.
2. Give each of your class members a prospect to contact, then check up on them the following Sunday to see if they have made the contact.

F. **Phone every prospect.**
  1. During a campaign, phone every prospect on your list, every week.
  2. Extend to each a friendly welcome, giving the time, place and lesson topic.

G. **Send mail to every prospect.**
  1. During a campaign, mail every prospect a postcard or letter, inviting them to Sunday School.
  2. A personal note, sent first class, works great.

H. **Visit every prospect.**
  1. Visitation puts the 'Go' in Gospel, carrying the message to every person.
  2. After you have phoned every prospect, a visit to their home will convince them of your love.
  3. In fact, during a Sunday School campaign you should visit every prospect every week.

I. **Be enthusiastic.**
  1. Enthusiasm is caught not taught!
  2. Be enthusiastic in your prayer to God for divine power.
  3. Be enthusiastic in presenting your program to your pupils.
     a. You have the greatest program . . . be enthusiastic!
     b. You have the greatest purpose . . . be enthusiastic!
     c. You have the greatest people . . . be enthusiastic!
     d. You have the greatest power . . . be enthusiastic!
     e. You have the greatest potential . . . be enthusiastic!

J. **Motivate your students to bring visitors.**
  1. We must have laborers.
  2. The biggest problem in the work of God is not finances, not buildings, not space, not equipment. The biggest problem is always, and will always be,

and has always been laborers. That is the number one thing to be conquered.

    3. That is what Jesus revealed to us when He said, *"Pray ye therefore the Lord of the harvest."* The harvest is great, but the laborers are few.

K. Have a contest in your class.

    1. During a Sunday School campaign every class should have their own campaign within the class.

    2. When there is not a campaign each class should have some type of promotion to get the students to:

        a. Come to Sunday School faithfully

        b. Bring their Bible

        c. Do their lesson

        d. Say their memory verse

        e. Bring an offering

        f. Bring a visitor

L. Determine to pay the price to reach the goal.

    1. The difference between dreamers and goal-reachers is the willingness of the 'reacher' to pay the price to do it.

    2. If you want to have an increase in your Sunday School class, that means there must be a willingness to pay the price to reach the goal.

    3. What are you willing to pay?

VI. What Are the Results Of Reaching a Set Goal?

  A. The results of reaching a set goal gives:

    1. A sense of achievement

    2. A feeling of satisfaction

    3. A blessing from the Lord of a job well done.

B. Reaching a goal is a method of measuring success. But, most importantly we will see souls saved and the Sunday School and Church grow.

LEARNING EXERCISE #2

INSTRUCTIONS: Fill in the blanks from the section you have just read.

1. After setting a goal, an equally difficult task lies in how to _____ the set goal.

2. Attainment requires a specific goal within _____ along with an explicit _____ for arriving there.

3. List twelve ways to reach your goal:
    a. _____
    b. _____
    c. _____
    d. _____
    e. _____
    f. _____
    g. _____
    h. _____
    i. _____
    j. _____
    k. _____
    l. _____

4. The results of reaching a set goal gives a sense of _____; it gives a feeling of _____; it gives a _____ from the Lord of a job well done.

5. _____ a goal is a method of measuring success.

6. But most importantly by reaching goals we will see souls _____ and the Sunday School and Church _____.

CHAPTER REVIEW (For *Certificate of Completion*)

INSTRUCTIONS: Write 'T" if the sentence is true, 'F' if the sentence is false.

1. _____ In order to build your Sunday School class you must set goals.
2. _____ A goal is a deliberate, premeditated, intentional aim that we seek to accomplish.
3. _____ A goal ought not be beyond accomplishment, it ought not be complicated, yet it ought not be too simple.
4. _____ An aim takes awareness of individual needs, and it takes knowledge of the ensuing course.
5. _____ Everyone who teaches a Sunday School class does not need to set a goal.
6. _____ It is not easier to make decisions when you know what you are trying to accomplish for the Lord.
7. _____ The following are reasons for setting goals: confidence building; save time; provide a sense of order.
8. _____ A teacher needs first to set long term goals.
9. _____ Goals must be written down.
10. _____ Goals must be broad.
11. _____ Goals must have time limits that are measurable.
12. _____ Goals must be published, stated openly, shared.
13. _____ After setting a goal, an equally difficult task lies in how to accomplish the set goal.

14. _____ Attainment requires a specific goal within reach along with an explicit plan for arriving there.

15. _____ The following are ways to reach your goal: Be enthusiastic; Use a numerical goal; Pray every day; Do all the work yourself.

16. _____ To reach your goal you should set a goal for finding new prospects.

17. _____ To reach your goal you should motivate your students to bring visitors.

18. _____ To reach your goal you must determine to pay the price.

19. _____ To reach your goal you must set a numerical goal.

20. _____ To reach your goal you only have to pray.

21. _____ The results of reaching a set goal gives a sense of achievement: it gives a feeling of satisfaction; it gives a blessing from the Lord of a job well done.

22. _____ Reaching a goal is a method of measuring success.

23. _____ Most importantly by reaching goals we will see souls saved and the Sunday School and Church grow.

CHAPTER TWELVE
HOW TO LEAD A PERSON TO CHRIST

I. INTRODUCTION

A child came forward in one of our church services. I asked him why he came. He said he wanted to get saved. I asked if he had ever been saved before and he replied, *"I've been saved seven times."*

One adult Christian woman relates how she responded to every invitation given to a group of children when she was a child. She says, *"There must be at least a dozen evangelists who count me as one of their converts, but it was not until years later that I actually knew what it meant to be a Christian."*

One four-year-old girl was watching a medical program on television with her parents. During the heart operation which was shown, she saw the doctors carefully lift out the patient's heart. At that moment she asked, *"Daddy, is he giving his heart to Jesus?"*

Why do children say such things? Can they really know that they are saved? It is possible for a child to be sure of his salvation just as much as an adult. The Bible says it is a child-like faith, so it's actually easier for a child to get saved than an adult.

II. Why Does A Child or Adult Talk About Being Saved More Than Once?

    A.   He does not understand the terminology that he hears.

        1.   First, he is told that he must be saved; then that he must let Jesus into his heart; next, he must give his heart to Jesus; then he must trust Jesus.

        2.   Each time he hears a new expression, he thinks he must respond. Thus he "goes forward" every time an invitation is expressed differently from what he last heard.

    B.   He is frightened into a decision.

        1.   Of course, a child or adult should know that there is a hell, but he needs to understand that Jesus died not

only to save him from hell, but also to keep him from sin now.

    2. When a child or adult makes a decision on the basis of fear alone, the scare may soon wear off, and soon he wonders if the whole experience was just something exciting for the moment.

C. He does not understand what sin is; therefore he really sees no need for a Savior.

D. He does not realize that he needs to make his decision to accept Christ as his Savior only once.

    1. Everybody tells him that he needs to accept Jesus; therefore he thinks he'd better do it each time someone says that he must.

    2. He needs to realize that once he accepts Jesus as his Savior he is in God's family, and that just as he came into his parents' family once, he comes into God's family once.

E. He may, at the time he goes forward, feel guilty of one particular sin that he has done. He asks forgiveness for this one misdeed, mistaking this experience for salvation. Then when he sins again, he thinks he must be saved again.

F. He goes for a reward. Sometimes a gift is promised to all those who come to receive Christ as Savior.

G. He follows the crowd. He comes forward to receive Christ because others went forward.

H. He wants to please someone. Many times both children and adults come forward simply to please a friend, relative or teacher.

I. He had no one teach him after he did accept Christ.

    1. Many children and adults do actually accept Christ as their Savior, but they are left without further direction and teaching.

    2. They don't read the Bible.

    3. They have questions but no one answers them.

4. No one helps them see how the Christian life differs from other lives.
5. No one teaches them how to pray.
6. Before long, they doubt or even forget their experience.

III. Giving An Invitation In Sunday School
A. Give an invitation after every lesson.
1. An effective way to give any invitation is to have the students close their eyes and bow their heads, and ask those who want to be saved to raise their hands.
2. This lets you know the ones who are under the conviction of the Holy Spirit.
3. Those who raise their hands should be counseled immediately.
B. Make the invitation clear, so that the student knows to what he is responding. A child's mind easily wanders, and he may respond just because other children do, especially if he does not clearly understand the issue.

IV. Explaining the Plan Of Salvation
A. Talk with the student individually and ask him why he came forward or raised his hand at the invitation.

If he or she responds with 'I don't know," then children should be sent back to their seat.
1. Teens and adults should have the invitation explained to them again.
2. If the child responds to accept Christ, ask him if he has accepted Him before.
3. If he or she has, ask him why the child wants to do it again.
4. You need to decide whether the child needs assurance or salvation.
5. If in doubt, deal with salvation.

B. Ask them if they know what sin is and to explain it to you. If a child does not know what sin is they are not ready to be saved.

C. Ask them if they have ever sinned.
1. The Bible says everyone is a sinner.
2. Romans 3:23, *"For all have sinned, and come short of the glory of God;"*

D. Tell them we cannot save ourselves by good works
1. Romans 3:28, *"Therefore we conclude that a man is justified by faith without the deeds of the law."*
2. Titus 3:5, *"Not by works of righteousness which we have done, but according to his mercy he saved us, by the washing of regeneration, and renewing of the Holy Ghost;"*

E. Explain that we are sinners and need to be saved but can't save ourselves.
1. Therefore, Jesus died on the cross to pay for our sins and save us.
2. Romans 5:8, *"But God commendeth his love toward us, in that, while we were yet sinners, Christ died for us."*

F. Show them that God has given us a choice:
1. To accept Christ
2. Or pay the penalty for our sin ourselves in hell
3. Romans 6:23, *"For the wages of sin is death; but the gift of God is eternal life through Jesus Christ our Lord."*

G. Finally, ask if they would like to receive Christ as Savior for the gift of eternal life.

If his answer is yes, then say, 'You must call upon the Lord to forgive your sin and save you.
1. Romans 10:13, *"For whosoever shall call upon the name of the Lord shall be saved."* Ephesians 2:8,9, *"For by grace are ye saved through faith; and that not of yourselves: it is the gift of God: Not of works, lest any man should boast."*

H. Next, lead them in the sinner's prayer.

1. Say to him, *"If this is what you really want to do I can lead us in prayer and we can tell God what you just told me."*

2. Pray for them to understand, repent and believe.

3. Pray with him, leading him in a short phrase at a time. The following is an example: *"Pray this prayer after me if you want to know that you have eternal life. Believe it in your heart and pray it to God in heaven. Pray it out loud, >>> Dear Lord, I know that I am a sinner and I cannot save myself. I believe that you died, were buried, and rose again to save me from my sin. I'm trusting you this minute to save me and give me the gift of eternal life. Thank you for saving me."*

I. Pray for this assurance of salvation.

J. Give some verses for assurance of salvation

1. 1 John 5:13, *"These things have I written unto you that believe on the name of the Son of God;* **that ye may know** *that ye have eternal life, and that ye may believe on the name of the Son of God."*

2. John 6:47, *"Verily, verily, I say unto you, He that believeth on me hath everlasting life."*

K. Choose your terminology carefully and avoid symbolism.

1. Use words a child can understand.

2. When you talk with the children, **do not** use phrases such as *"ask Jesus to come into your heart," "give you heart to Christ," "your heart is dark with sin," "Jesus is knocking at the door of your heart."*

    Instead, use biblical words such as "trust," "receive," "believe," and "accept."

V. **The Follow-up After Salvation**
   A. When students accept Christ as Savior, the teacher's job is not done. A big job is just begun.
      1. The students need to be taught.
      2. They should be visited.
      3. They need to learn to pray, to read the Bible, and to live a life pleasing to God.
      4. Many are sent away, after accepting Christ, with these words, *"Now you are a Christian, you must pray and read your Bible every day."* That is all the followup they get from the one who led them to Christ.
   B. To help students remember this important decision in their lives:
      1. Have them write in their Bible the date they were saved and the verses used.
      2. If they don't have a Bible, give them one.
   C. Encourage them to tell their family of this decision as soon as they get home and tell the class the next week.

LEARNING EXERCISE #1

INSTRUCTIONS: Fill in the blanks from the section you have just read.

1. List nine reasons why a person talks about being saved more than once:

   a. _____
   b. _____
   c. _____
   d. _____
   e. _____
   f. _____
   g. _____
   h. _____
   i. _____

2. Give an invitation after every _____ .

3. An effective way to give an invitation is to have the students _____ and _____ , and ask those who want to be saved to _____ .

4. Make the invitation _____ .

5. Explain the nine steps in the plan of salvation.
    a. _____
    b. _____
    c. _____
    d. _____
    e. _____
    f. _____
    g. _____
    h. _____
    i. _____

6. Choose your _____ carefully and avoid _____ .

7. When you talk with children, do not use phrases such as "_____ , _____ , _____ ."

8. When a student accepts Christ as Savior, the teachers job is _____ .

9. List five things a new Christian needs:
    a. _____
    b. _____
    c. _____
    d. _____
    e. _____

10. To help students remember this important decision in their lives, have them write in their Bible the _____ they were saved and the _____ used.

11. If they don't have a _____ give them one.

12. Encourage them to tell their _____ of this decision as soon as they get home.

CHAPTER REVIEW (For *Certificate of Completion*)

INSTRUCTIONS: Write 'T" if the sentence is true, 'F' if the sentence is false.

1. _____ The following reasons are why a person talks about being saved more than once: He goes for a reward; He follows the crowd; He wants to please someone; He lost his salvation.

2. _____ Teachers should give an invitation after every lesson.

3. _____ An effective way to give an invitation is to ask each student in front of the class.

4. _____ The teacher should make the invitation clear.

5. _____ The first step in leading a student to Christ is to talk with them individually and ask them why they came or raised their hand.

6. _____ If a student doesn't know what sin is he can't be saved.

7. _____ The teacher should ask the student if they have ever sinned.

8. _____ We cannot save ourselves by good works.

9. _____ The teacher must explain that we are sinners and need to be saved but can't save ourselves, so Jesus died on the cross to pay for our sins and save us.

10. _____ God has given us a choice to accept Christ or pay the penalty for our sin ourselves in hell.

11. _____ The teacher should not ask them if they would like to receive Christ as Savior.

12. _____ The teacher should lead the student in the sinner's prayer.

13. _____ Two verses of assurance are: 1 John 5:13; John 6:47.

14. _____ In leading a soul to Christ you should choose your terminology carefully and avoid symbolism.

15. _____ When you talk with children use phrases such as "ask Jesus to come into your heart."

16. _____ When a student accepts Christ as Savior, the teacher's job is not done.

17. _____ The following things are needed by a new Christian: to be visited; to be taught; to pray, to read the Bible; to live a life pleasing to God.

18. _____ To help students remember their salvation decision in their life, have them write in their Bible the date they were saved and the verses used.

19. _____ If a new convert doesn't have a Bible, give him one.

20. _____ You should encourage a new convert to tell their family of their decision as soon as they get home.

CHAPTER THIRTEEN
HOW TO EVALUATE YOUR TEACHING

I. Introduction

A parent came to me complaining that her daughter didn't like her Sunday School class; she said her daughter said it was boring. I told the mother I would have a talk with the teacher.

Not long after I spoke with the mother, I casually one Sunday asked the teacher how her class was going. She replied, *"Great, the kids just love the class!"*

I thought, "something is wrong here." Somebody surely was not evaluating the class properly. So I began to observe the class from a distance. After about a month, I found that the student was right. The class was declining. The teacher was not studying her lessons (I found her teacher's manual left in the classroom).

When I was in seminary I took a course called homiletics. It was designed to help us develop our skill of preaching. Each student would preach a sermon to the class; while the rest of the class would evaluate their preaching.

The evaluation of our preaching would help us to see things that we ourselves could not see. The purpose of the evaluation was then to help us improve our preaching gift.

Sunday School teachers need to be evaluated so they can improve their teaching gift.

Evaluation of teaching is important. Most teachers are surprised to discover how little knowledge is actually retained by their students. Hence, there is a vital need to evaluate teaching methods and emphasis and to review lessons.

Sooner or later every teacher's effectiveness will be judged, not only by people, but also by God. 1 Corinthians 3:1-15 indicates that those who teach cannot escape the testing of their work and workmanship.

There are three basic ways you can evaluate your teaching: by student evaluation, self-evaluation and superintendent or leader evaluation.

II. Student Evaluation

A. You can evaluate your teaching by how much knowledge students retain. This can be done by oral participation or written examinations.

B. Much of the evaluation can be done by means of well conducted oral participation.

1. This should be more than a mere repetition of exact words or phrases.

2. Student knowledge is examined to determine whether it is clear or confused.

3. Students should be encouraged to say in their own way what they understand to be the truth.

4. If teachers are to obtain a true picture of students' understanding, the questions asked should be thorough, searching, correct, and inspiring.

5. This approach requires preparation by the teacher as well as the student.

C. Written examinations are an accepted part of general education.

1. Many persons have had unhappy experiences with them.

2. You should use written tests with caution and discretion.

D. Many people relate examinations to wearisome, last minute cramming or the painful experience of trying to put on paper what has been laboriously or hurriedly memorized.

1. They are concerned about unanticipated questions and unanswerable problems.

2. Sunday School teachers and students alike have avoided testing in general.

3. If teaching is taken seriously, and is earnest, thoughtful, and skillful, various methods of testing can be used effectively.

            4. A well designed examination challenges students to rethink what they have learned and to express their learning in a life-related context.

            5. One way of evaluating by oral participation and written exams is to put them in the form of a game.

    E. To even say the words 'test' or 'exam' evokes fear in the minds of many people.

III. **Self Evaluation**
    A. Someone has said you are your own worst critic.

        If you desire to be the best teacher that you can be for the glory of the Lord, then at least twice a year you should take the 'Self-Rating Teacher's Evaluation."

            1. It is important that you answer honestly.

            2. This is a simple test for Sunday School teachers, which shows how efficient you are as a Sunday School teacher.

            3. This has been adapted from Scripture Press:

SELF-RATING TEACHER'S EVALUATION

INSTRUCTIONS: Answer the following questions "Yes" or "No."

1. _____ Do you pray daily for your class and department?

2. _____ Are you faithful in attendance, rain or shine?

3. _____ Do you arrive fifteen minutes before class begins to spend time listening to your pupils?

4. _____ Do you sit with your class during opening worship, gladly taking part?

5. _____ Do you make records promptly, getting records to the secretary without class interruption?

6. _____ Do you have a clear overall view of the entire quarter's lessons?

7. _____ Can you put into one brief sentence your teaching aim for each Sunday?

8. _____ Do your pupils understand that the lesson is from the Bible, not just a quarterly?

9. _____ Do you use a vocabulary your pupils understand?

10. _____ Do you ask questions and encourage your pupils to comment freely when the group will benefit?

11. _____ Have you already started preparing next week's lesson by Tuesday of each week?

12. _____ If something funny happens in class, do you join in the laugh and use the incident to get back into the lesson?

13. _____ Can you put a talkative pupil in his place without his resenting it?

Comment   Grade

1. **Lesson plan**
    a. Clear and easy to follow
    b. Teachability, organization
2. **Teaching process**
    a. Approach
        (1) gain attention
        (2) length
    b. Body
        (1) organized
        (2) clear
        (3) scriptural; Bible based
        (4) adequate application

(5) interest maintained

(6) taken from unknown to known

   c. Conclusion

(1) goals reached

(2) student challenged

(3) clear and concise

   d. Decision for action

(1) student response

(2) adequate carryover

1. **Teaching Method**
    a. Audio - visuals
    b. Variety
    c. Pupil involvement
    d. Levels of learning

2. **The Teacher**
    a. Physical appearance
    b. Voice monotone, etc.
    c. Enthusiasm
    d. Grammar
    e. Class discipline

LEARNING EXERCISE #1

INSTRUCTIONS: Fill in the blanks from the section you have just read.

1. Sunday School teachers need to be evaluated so they can _____ their teaching gift.

2. Evaluation of teaching is _____ .

3. Most teachers are surprised to discover how little knowledge is actually _____ by their students.

4. Sooner or later every teacher's effectiveness will be judged, not only by _____ but also by_____ .

5. List the three basic ways you can evaluate your teaching:

   a. _____

   b. _____

   c. _____

6. You can evaluate your teaching by how much knowledge students retain; this can be done _____ or _____ .

7. If teachers are to obtain a true picture of student's understanding, the questions asked should be _____, _____ , _____ , and _____ .

8. You should use written tests with _____ and _____ .

9. One way of evaluating by oral participation and written exams is to put them in the form of a _____ .

10. To even say the words 'test' or 'exam' evokes fear in the _____ .

11. Someone has said you are your own _____ .

12. If you desire to be the _____ teacher that you can be for the glory of the Lord, then at least _____ a year you should take the 'Self-Rating Teacher's Evaluation."

13. At least _____ a year the Sunday School superintendent should observe every class in the Sunday School.

14. Every teacher who truly desires to be the best teacher they can for the Lord will not take _____ to the superintendent or another qualified leader observing their class and showing them how they can make _____ .

15. Teachers should also take the _____ in a God-pleasing, Christ-honoring way.

16. Teachers should be _____ to have someone come into their class and make _____ to make their class _____ .

CHAPTER REVIEW (For *Certificate of Completion*)
INSTRUCTIONS: Write 'T" if the sentence is true, 'F" if the sentence is false.

1. _____ Sunday School teachers don't need to be evaluated.
2. _____ Evaluation of teaching is important.
3. _____ Most teachers are surprised to discover how little knowledge is actually retained by their students.
4. _____ Sooner or later every teacher's effectiveness will be judged, not only by others, but also by God.
5. _____ There are only two basic ways to evaluate your teaching.
6. _____ You can evaluate your teaching by how much knowledge students retain, this can be done by oral participation or written examination.
7. _____ If teachers are to obtain a true picture of students' understanding, the questions asked should be thorough, searching, incorrect, and inspiring.
8. _____ Sunday School teachers should use written tests with caution and discretion.
9. _____ One way of evaluating by oral participation and written exams is to put them in the form of a game.
10. _____ To even say the words 'test' or 'exam"\' evokes fear in the minds of many people.
11. _____ You are your own worst critic.

12. _____ At least twice a year you should take the 'SelfRating Teacher's Evaluation."

13. _____ At least once a year the Sunday School Superintendent should observe every class in the Sunday School.

14. _____ Every teacher who truly desires to be the best teacher they can be for the Lord will not take offence to the superintendent observing their class.

15. _____ Teachers should be eager to have someone come into their class and make suggestions to make their class better.

FINAL REVIEW

INSTRUCTIONS: Write "T" if the sentence is true, "F" if the sentence is false.

1. _____ The average Sunday School teacher has had lots of teaching experience.

2. _____ The average Sunday School teacher is one of the main reasons many Sunday Schools are not growing today.

3. _____ The average Sunday School teacher spends more than an hour a week in preparing her lesson.

4. _____ The average Sunday School teacher usually prepares their lesson on Saturday night.

5. _____ The average Sunday School teacher usually arrives late.

6. _____ The average Sunday School teacher makes little use of new methods or visuals; they teach the same way week after week.

7. _____ The aim and nature of Christian education necessitates born again teachers.

8. _____ An unsaved person, though maybe religious, does not know God and therefore is incapable of communicating the truth and will of God to others.

9. _____ Only a person who has been properly baptized and is a member of the local church he wishes to teach in can Scripturally carry out the Lord's commission.

10. _____ The Sunday School teacher must believe in the Bible as the inspired Word of God.

11. _____ The Sunday School teacher must be a doer of the Word and not just a hearer.

12. _____ The Sunday School teacher should try to live daily so that others may see Christ in them.

13. _____ The Sunday School teacher will pray and read their Bible once a week.

14. _____ The Sunday School teacher will be a soul winner.

15. _____ The Sunday School teacher can be late once in a while.

16. _____ It is clear from the Scripture that every believer has some gift.

17. _____ The gifts of apostleship, healing, tongues and prophecy were temporary gifts.

18. _____ The gift of teaching is a supernatural, spirit endowed ability to expound the truth of God.

19. _____ Each believer must discover whether or not God has given them a gift.

20. _____ If a person were gifted as a teacher before he was saved he should consider whether this may be his spiritual gift for edifying the church.

21. _____ A spiritual gift is an entrustment, as well as an enablement, and endowment.

22. _____ If a Christian has the teaching gift, he or she is not responsible to care for it as a steward would his master's household.

23. _____ There are three means by which one may develop his gift of teaching: observing others who have the gift, getting training and schooling in how to teach, and gaining teaching experience.

24. _____ Christian teachers will be anxious to do all they can to improve and make the best use of their gift.

25. _____ The Sunday School teacher must know the Lord personally.

26. _____ The single most important factor that influences learning is the life and personality of the teacher.

Final Review

27. _____ The effective teacher doesn't have to know the lesson thoroughly.

28. _____ Teachers should know more than they have time to teach, not just enough to fill the time.

29. _____ Attention and interest are directly related to motivation.

30. _____ Motivation facilitates learning.

31. _____ When pupils are motivated to learn, they learn more quickly and the results are more lasting.

32. _____ Language must have the same meaning for both teacher and student.

33. _____ Smaller children think figuratively.

34. _____ The truth to be taught must be learned through truth already known.

35. _____ Never find out what your pupils know of the subject you wish to teach them.

36. _____ It is enough for students to learn Bible facts.

37. _____ The pupil must reproduce in his own mind the truth to be learned.

38. _____ No lesson is fully learned until it is traced to its connections with life.

39. _____ The completion, test and confirmation of the work of teaching must be made by review and application.

40. _____ A review is more than repetition.

41. _____ Frequent repetitions are valuable to correct memorization and aid ready recall.

42. _____ Teachers should try to set aside a little time each day to study their Sunday School lesson.

43. _____ A little study each day is better than cramming.

44. _____ Teachers are not prepared to teach until they prepare themselves through prayer.

45. _____ The purpose of Sunday School teaching is not only to communicate content, but to teach for change.

46. _____ The aim of the lesson should be stated in specific terms, in one or two sentences.

47. _____ The aim is the goal of your teaching, it is what you want to see happen in your students' lives.

48. _____ One of the best ways to familiarize yourself with the passage to be taught is by reading the passage repeatedly.

49. _____ You should organize your Sunday School lesson around an outline.

50. _____ Teaching without a conclusion is like fishing without a hook.

51. _____ The purpose of an introduction is to bridge the gap between where the students are and where the lesson begins.

52. _____ A good introduction catches the attention of the student, creates a desire to learn, inspires action and becomes a point of contact.

53. _____ The key to a teacher's appearance is not to let anything detract from the Sunday School lesson.

54. _____ Anything that would cause a student's attention to be drawn away from the lesson should be eliminated.

55. _____ Your dress should be modest, conservative, in good taste and suited to the occasion.

56. _____ When you teach from a chair, you should sit up, not slouch forward or backward.

57. _____ Poise is the ability not only to be at ease when things are running smoothly, but to keep your head and come up unruffled when things are not.

58. _____ No introduction, regardless of how interesting it may be, is a success if it does not open the door to the lesson.

59. _____ You don't have to be sold on your story to make others sold on it.

60. _____ If you are not sincere, you won't fool anyone, especially children.

61. _____ If a story is worth telling at all, it is worth telling with all your heart.

62. _____ Enthusasm is a trait that is so powerful that it can be downright dangerous if used wrongly.

63. _____ Enthusiasm does not necessarily mean a lot of noise.

64. _____ The Master-Teacher approach is teacher-centered, relying mainly on the lecture method of teaching.

65. _____ The Guided Discovery Learning approach to teaching a Sunday School is a student-centered method.

66. _____ Sitting down when teaching causes one to hold his voice down, and allows a more personal eye to eye contact.

67. _____ Guided Discovery Learning encourages participation.

68. _____ Guided Discovery Learning is based upon the presupposition that people learn more through "hearing and doing" together than through simply hearing.

69. _____ A good teacher will spend no more than 50 to 60 percent of the time talking.

70. _____ Your outline is what you will use to keep the discussion on track.

71. _____ Brainstorming is a method of problem solving in which group members suggest in rapid fire order all the possible solutions they can think of.

72. _____ A case study is an account of a problem situation, including sufficient detail to make it possible for groups to analyze problems involved.

73. _____ Role playing is the rehearsed, dramatic enactment of a human conflict situation by two or more persons for the purpose of analysis by the group.

74. _____ Buzz groups discuss assigned problems, usually for the purpose of reporting back to the larger group.

75. _____ If a question is relevant at the point in the lesson when asked, answer it.

76. _____ A great fear of new teachers, especially working with adults is, "What if they ask a question to which I don't know the answer?"

77. _____ If a person becomes disruptive to the class, you will ultimately have to tell them privately after a class session they must give others an opportunity to participate.

78. _____ A learning aid is any device that helps teachers communicate more effectively with their students.

79. _____ Aids help capture and hold students' attention and make learning more rapid.

80. _____ Teens are concerned about their height, weight, hair styles and other appearance issues.

81. _____ To have an effective ministry to young adults, you must provide activities.

82. _____ Two and three-year-olds are dependent, self-centered, play alone, like friends and need attention.

Final Review 193

83. _____ A bleak, pessimistic spirit is common among senior adults.

84. _____ Nine, ten and eleven-year-olds are sometimes noisy and may push and shove occasionally.

85. _____ Good Sunday School teachers will have their class planned out.

86. _____ Class business should be limited basically to the announcements and taking roll.

87. _____ The Sunday School teacher should arrive one minute early to prepare the classroom and the pupil for the lesson.

88. _____ The teacher should properly meet and greet all visitors before the starting of the opening assembly.

89. _____ Teachers and leaders must not only instruct, but also exercise discipline.

90. _____ Children who are starving for love may misbehave.

91. _____ Being organized helps prevent the students from becoming overly restless.

92. _____ The teacher should try to handle problems, if possible, without stopping the class and interrupting the other students.

93. _____ You should never act exasperated in front of students.

94. _____ In order to build your Sunday School class you must set goals.

95. _____ A goal is a deliberate, premeditated, intentional aim that we seek to accomplish.

96. _____ If students don't know what sin is they can't be saved.

97. _____ In leading a soul to Christ you should choose your terminology carefully and avoid symbolism.

98. _____ Sunday School teachers don't need to be evaluated.

99. _____ Sooner or later every teacher's effectiveness will be judged, not only by men, but also by God.

100. _____ Studying this book has been very informative and helpful to me.

BIBLIOGRAPHY

1. Barrett, Ethel. *Story Telling It's Easy*. Grand Rapids: Zondervan Publishing House. 1968.

2. Bowman. *Straight Talks About Teaching in Today's Church*. Philadelphia: Westminster Press. 1967.

3. Brown, Lowell E. *Sunday School Standards*. Ventura: Gospel Light Publications. 1978.

4. Criswell, W. A. *Criswell's Guidebook For Pastors*. Nashville: Broadman Press. 1980.

5. Eavey, C. B. *Principles of Teaching for Christian Teachers*. Grand Rapids: Zondervan Publishing House. 1970.

6. Evangelical Teacher Training Association. *Teaching Techniques*. Wheaton: Evangelical Teacher Training Association. 1983.

7. Ford, Leroy. *A Primer For Teachers and Leaders*. Nashville: Broadman Press. 1963.

8. Gregory, John Milton. *The Seven Laws of Teaching*. Grand Rapids: Baker, 1954.

9. Hendricks, Howard G. *The Seven Laws of the Teacher*. Atlanta: Walk Thru the Bible Ministries, Inc. 1988.

10. Hyles, Jack. *The Hyles Sunday School Manual*. Murfreesboro: Sword of the Lord Publishers. 1969.

11. Knight, George. *Instant Cartoons for Church Newsletters*. Grand Rapids: Baker Book House. 1982.

12. Leavitt. *Teach With Success*. Seminary notes: Dr. Ben's class. 1976.

13. Miller, Vernon. *2's and 3's Teacher*. Schaumburg: Regular Baptist Press. 1992.

14. Miller, Vernon. *4's and 5's Teacher*. Schaumburg: Regular Baptist Press. 1992.

15. Miller, Vernon. *Primary Teacher*. Schaumburg: Regular Baptist Press. 1992.

16. Miller, Vernon. *Junior Teacher*. Schaumburg: Regular Baptist Press. 1992.

17. Miller, Vernon. *Youth Teacher.* Schaumburg: Regular Baptist Press. 1992.

18. Richard, Lawrence 0. *Creative Bible Teaching.* Chicago: Moody Press. 1970.

19 Schaffer, Ron. *The Sunday School Manual.* Franklin: Macedonia Evangelistic Association.

20 Sexton, Clarence. *Big Ideas For a Better Sunday School.* Chattanooga: Clarence G. Sexton. 1978.

21. Soderholm, Marjorie. *Explaining Salvation to Children.* Minneapolis: Free Church Publication, 1972.

22. Towns, Elmer. *Towns on Teacher Training.* Lynchburg: Church Growth Institute. 1989.

23. Towns, Elmer. *World's Largest Sunday School.* Nashville: Thomas Nelson, Inc. 1974.

24. Towns, Elmer. *The Complete Book of Church Growth.* Wheaton: Tyndale House Publishers Inc. 1981.

25. Willis, Wesley R. *Make Your Teaching Count.* Wheaton: Victor Books, 1991.

26. Zuck, Roy B. *Spiritual Power in Your Teaching.* Chicago: Moody Press, 1972.

27. Zuck, Roy B. and Getz, Gene A. *Adult Education In The Church.* Chicago: Moody Press. 1974.

ANSWER KEY for LEARNING EXERCISES

CHAPTER ONE ANSWER KEY
LEARNING EXERCISE #1:
1. average Sunday School
2. women
3. two
4. one
5. teaching
6. hour, week
7. Bible, quarterly
8. arrives late
9. the same way
10. self-satisfaction

CHAPTER TWO ANSWER KEY
LEARNING EXERCISE #1:
1. saved, baptized
2. say
3. follower
4. example
5. saved
6. called, Christian
7. faith in Jesus Christ
8. Christian, Christian
9. aim
10. nature
11. incapable, truth
12. influence
13. local church

14. baptized, member
15. yes or no (if no, you need to get this taken care of)

LEARNING EXERCISE #2:
1. Scripture
2. Jesus Christ
3. immersion
4. inspired Word of God
5. doer, hearer
6. tithes, offerings
7. liquor, tobacco
8. Christ
9. class
10. study
11. prospects, visitors, absentees
12. superintendent
13. know Christ
14. love
15. time
16. lean, guide
17. gift of teaching

CHAPTER THREE ANSWER KEY
LEARNING EXERCISE #1
1. spiritual gifts
2. teachers
3. general
4. gift
5. diversity, unity

6. sixteen
7. divine, sovereignly
8. each one
9. permanent, temporary
10. Permanent: Temporary:
    teaching   apostleship
    evangelism   prophecy
    pastoring   performing miracles
    exhorting   healing
    giving   tongues
    showing mercy   interpreting tongues
    helping
    administering
    discerning spirits
    faith
11. a. edifying body of Christ
    b. ascribing glory to the Lord
12. Christian education
13. preaching
14. edifying
15. teaching gift
16. supernatural ability
17. expound
18. natural birth
19. spiritual gifts
20. a. enhance
    b. channel
    c. quicken

LEARNING EXERCISE #2:

1. a. discover
   b. develop
   c. exercise
2. the gift of teaching
3. unaware
4. a. they have not been instructed about spiritual gifts
   b. they are out of fellowship with the Lord
5. before, consider
6. several capacities
7. spiritual results, blessings
8. center, will
9. first step
10. three
11. stewardship
12. entrustment, enablement, endowment
13. responsible
14. a. observing others who have the gift of teaching
    b. getting training and schooling in how to teach
    c. gaining teaching experience
15. anxious, improve

CHAPTER FOUR ANSWER KEY

LEARNING EXERCISE #1:

1. personally
2. word, Spirit
3. life, personality
4. a. Teaching techniques are of little use unless they are used by one through whose life the truth and love of God radiate.
   b. Christian truths are better understood when seen in life.
   c. Lives are impressed and changed more by truths they see demonstrated than those that merely hear spoken.
5. intimately
6. learning
7. needs
8. thoroughly
9. fill the time
10. ease

LEARNING EXERCISE #2:

1. learned
2. attention
3. genuine interest
4. attention, interest
5. desirable, desired
6. learning
7. lasting
8. a. internal
   b. external

9.
   a. protect me: self-perservation
   b. exalt me: recognition
   c. accept me: social acceptance
   d. love me: affection
10.
   a. bandwagon
   b. statistics
   c. praise
   d. rebuke
   e. testimony
   f. illustration
   g. peer pressure

LEARNING EXERCISE #3:

1. teacher
2. understood
3. meaning
4. vocabulary
5. language of the students
6. church
7. students
8. simplicity
9. illustration
10. literally

LEARNING EXERCISE #4:

1. known
2. known, familiar
3. concept
4. mastered, starting
5. new knowledge

6. cloud, shadow
7. subject
8. knowledge, experience
9. easily, naturally
10. common, familiar

LEARNING EXERCISE #5:
1. self activities
2. stimulates
3. Bible facts
4. live
5. think
6. independent
7. self learning
8. independent study
9. ask
10. a. What
    b. Why
    c. How

LEARNING EXERCISE #6:
1. mind
2. memorization, repetition
3. truth
4. pupil, teacher
5. learned
6. application
7. Sunday School
8. Finds a use for what they have learned; applies their knowledge to practical everyday life.

LEARNING EXERCISE #7:

1. review, application
2. repetition
3. intelligent
4. rethinking
5. itself
6. truths, meanings
7. repetitions
8. memory
9. familiarizes, strengthens
10. a. to perfect knowledge
    b. to confirm knowledge
    c. to render the knowledge ready and useful
11. a. power of repetition
    b. lapse of time changes point of view
    c. survey of lesson from a new standpoint
    d. finding of fresh truth and new meaning
    e. becomes woven into the very fabric of thought
12. a. More than mere repetition
    b. Thorough restudy of the lessons; a careful resurvey
    c. Interesting, challenging

CHAPTER FIVE ANSWER KEY

LEARNING EXERCISE #1:

1. lesson
2. time
3. each day
4. students
5. cramming
6. answers may vary

    a. Sunday afternoon. Evaluate the day's lesson. Read over the next lesson.

    b. Monday-Wednesday. Study the Bible, using the teacher's manual and other helps.

    c. Thursday-Friday. Write out the actual lesson with aim, method, and materials.

    d. Saturday. Gather material and teaching aids. Review briefly.

    e. Sunday morning. Review briefly and teach the lesson.

LEARNING EXERCISE #2:

1. prayer
2. pupils
3. study, preparation
4. teachable
5.
    a. Pray for a teachable spirit

    b. Pray for the teaching ministry of the Holy Spirit

    c. Pray for guidance in lesson preparation

    d. Pray for each student

LEARNING EXERCISE #3:

1. whole, whole
2. important
3. overview
4. teaching it
5. preceding, following

LEARNING EXERCISE #4:

1. content
2. purpose
3. truth, aim
4. supplementation
5. pupils

LEARNING EXERCISE #5:

1. change
2. pupils to make
3. specific
4. aim
5.
   a. Guides Bible study
   b. Gives unity, order, and efficiency to teaching.
   c. Gives teachers confidence in the classroom.
   d. Helps teachers use time efficiently
   e. Helps teachers select teaching aids and methods
   f. Helps teachers evaluate a lesson

LEARNING EXERCISE #6:

1. Word
2. start
3. repeatedly
4. easy
5. are, be
6. a. Bible concordance
   b. Bible dictionary
   c. Bible commentary

LEARNING EXERCISE #7:

1. word for word
2. outline
3. study
4. presentation
5. seeds, plants

LEARNING EXERCISE #8:

1. hook
2. conclusion
3. aim
4. stops
5. personally
6. lag
7. apologizing
8. summarize

LEARNING EXERCISE #9:

1. introduction
2. bridge the gap
3. attention
4. promise
5. answers may vary
    a. a story from everyday life
    b. a story from the Scriptures
    c. a current event
    d. a question
    e. a visual aid
    f. a filmstrip or slides
    g. a quotation
    h. a picture that reflects the lesson
    i. a drawing on the chalkboard

LEARNING EXERCISE #10:

1. several revisions
2. material
3. arise
4. times
5. last review

CHAPTER SIX ANSWER KEY
LEARNING EXERCISE #1:

1. detract
2. eliminated
3. modest
4. attractive
5. groomed
6. delivered
7. little things
8. a. general appearance
   b. breathcontrol
   c. voice
9. sit up
10. naturally
11. a. Don't overdo.
    b. Don't become addicted to one gesture.
    c. Don't become known for eccentric gestures.
12. gestures, posture
13. mastered
14. poise
15. unruffled

LEARNING EXERCISE #2:

1. first sentence
2. introduction
3. approach
4. attitudes, interest
5. a. brought by parents

       b. enjoy the fellowship
       c. desire to study the Word of God
6. a. establish a point of contact
    b. arouse interest in learning
    c. focus their attention on the lesson
7. success
8. a. current events
    b. stories and illustrations
    c. provocative questions
    d. visuals

LEARNING EXERCISE #3:

1. attitudes
2. prayer, practice
3. a. Salesmanship
    b. Sincerity
    c. Earnestness
    d. Wholeheartedness
    e. Enthusiasm
    f. Animation
    g. A Broken Heart
    h. Be Yourself
4. sold, sell
5. degree
6. sincere
7. earnest
8. Word of God
9. heart
10. Enthusiasm
11. noise

12. animation
13. tragedy
14. delivery
15. art

CHAPTER SEVEN ANSWER KEY
LEARNING EXERCISE #1:

1. teacher-centered
2. student-centered
3. personal
4. guiding, preaching
5. members
6. hearing, doing
7. 90 percent
8. 50-60 percent
9. participation
10. question
11. a. think
    b. read
    c. study
    d. ponder
    e. reason
12. Guided Discovery Learning
13. opinion
14. objective
15. outline

LEARNING EXERCISE #2:

1. Lecturing
2. Group discussion
3. a. share ideas
   b. identify problems
   c. find solutions
4. prepared questions
5. possible solutions
6. analyze problems
7. case
8. role playing
9. groups
10. group

LEARNING EXERCISE #3:

1. relevant
2. a. Postpone
   b. Preclude
   c. Promptly answer
   d. Promise to research and return
3. answer
4. I don't know, but I'll find out and tell you next week.
5. everything
6. a. Do not call on a specific person to pray without first having asked their permission.
   b. Do not ask direct questions.
   c. Do not ask a visitor a question or to read.
7. conducted

8. privately
9. ask
10. Bible study
11. every
12. church, Bible study

LEARNING EXERCISE #4:

1. learning aid
2. instruction
3. language barrier
4. attention, learning
5. alive
6. a. Habit, use only what is most comfortable and familiar.
   b. Aids, usually take extra time and planning to prepare and require certain skills in using equipment.
   c. Many aids, especially audiovisuals, do involve some expense for equipment and materials.
7. effective, ineffective, skill

CHAPTER EIGHT ANSWER KEY
LEARNING EXERCISE #1:

1. a. He is active
   b. He can use his hands
   c. He is gaining coordination
   d. He has short endurance
   e. His voice is still developing
   f. He likes to imitate

2.
  a. They are inquisitive
  b. They can learn
  c. They have a short attention span
  d. They believe their teacher
  e. They have a poor memory
  f. They think in small numbers
  g. They do not understand symbolism
  h. They use his senses
  i. They like repetition
3.
  a. They is fearful
  b. They respond to love
  c. They need security
  d. They need acceptance
  e. They are sensitive
  f. They say no
4.
  a. They are dependent
  b. They are self-centered
  c. They play alone
  d. They like friends
  e. They need attention
5.
  a. They want to pray
  b. They are interested in the Bible
  c. They want to know about God
  d. They sense the wonders of God
  e. They are usually not ready to receive Christ as Savior

LEARNING EXERCISE #2:
1. boundless
2. Bible story

Answer Key for Learning Exercises   *215*

3. crayons
4. active, quiet
5. a. Their attention span is increasing
   b. They love to ask questions
   c. Their vocabulary is increasing and speaks in simple sentences
   d. They like to use his imagination
   e. They learn through imitation
6. easily upset
7. calm, calm, abrupt
8. mothers, fathers
9. way
10. approval, sympathy
11. a. They enjoy playing with other children
    b. They are self-centered
12. a. They think of God in a personal way
    b. They understand the difference between doing right and doing wrong
    c. They can understand the Bible is God's special book
    d. They may be ready to accept Christ as their Savior

LEARNING EXERCISE #3:

1. taller, thinner
2. work, play
3. memorizing, writing, coloring, craft
4. read, write
5. memories

6. words, numbers
7. reason, conclusions
8. symbolism
9. impatient
10. obedience
11. talk
12. selfish, pray
13. spiritual things
14. good

LEARNING EXERCISE #4:
1. strong, healthy, active, energy
2. height
3. outdoors
4. push, shove
5. sharp
6. read, write
7. history, geography
8. Thinking, reasoning
9. accepted
10. Behavior
11. follow
12. Resistance
13. responsibility
14. macho, sophisticated
15. quick-tempered
16. good time
17. accept
18. sin
19. Lord

Answer Key for Learning Exercises

LEARNING EXERCISE #5:

1. height, weight, hair
2. grown
3. anxiety
4. self-image
5. history, future
6. today
7. needs, needs
8. motivator
9. alive, moving
10. often
11. peer
12. embarrass
13. on the spot
14. volunteers
15. 85, 18
16. spiritual decisions

LEARNING EXERCISE #6:

1. activities
2. positive, fun, exciting, well-studied, motivator and leader
3. follow
4. education
5.
    a. Selecting a mate
    b. Learning to live with a marriage partner
    c. Starting a family
    d. Rearing children
    e. Managing a home.

		f.	Getting started in an occupation.

   f.   Getting started in an occupation.
   g.   Taking on civic responsibility.
   h.   Finding a congenial social group.
6. a. self
   b. others
   c. life
7. ministering to them
8. service

LEARNING EXERCISE #7:

1. biological, physical
2. acuity
3. physically
4. small
5. service
6. biological changes
7. attitude
8. a. Teach the Bible creatively and relevantly.
   b. Provide instruction and guidance on potential issues of adult life.
   c. Offer instruction and counsel on how middle adults can adjust to difficult circumstances of life.
   d. Encourage adults to plan and participate in adult size social and recreational activities.

LEARNING EXERCISE #8:

1. decline
2. physical problems

3. educational
4. Social
5. marital relationships
6. aged
7. one third
8.
   a. Some find the curriculum and teaching irrelevant to their current needs.
   b. Others find them to be repetition of what they have "always had" in lessons during previous stages of the life cycle.
   c. Some face complications of physical health, problems of transportation, or difficulties in sitting through two hours of activities.
   d. Some have either drifted from their faith or never truly possessed it.

LEARNING EXERCISE #9:
1. social
2.
   a. aloneness
   b. loneliness
   c. sexuality
3. attitude
4. church
5. sympathy, understanding, love

CHAPTER NINE ANSWER KEY
LEARNING EXERCISE #1:
1. planned out
2. fifteen

3. visitors
4. ten
5. greet
6. fellowship, bond
7. announcements, taking roll
8. prayer list
9. never
10. former, integrated
11. are, take
12. I'm starting, come to order
13. raise of hands
14. spot
15. decision
16. clean up

CHAPTER TEN ANSWER KEY
LEARNING EXERCISE #1:

1. past
2. change lives
3. law, order
4. confusion, chaos
5. trained in orderliness
6. nurture, admonition
7. instruction, discipline
8. discipline
9. disorder
10. happen
11. root
12. conception, choice, conduct
13. Satan

Answer Key for Learning Exercises 221

14. pupils
15. a. poor vision
    b. retardation
    c. hearing problems
    d. sickness
16. a. Human beings are sinners by nature.
    b. Satan is against the work of God.
    c. Bad home situations.
    d. Physical disabilities.
    e. No instruction on proper behavior.
    f. Permissive public schools.
    g. Fear.
    h. They are starving for love.

LEARNING EXERCISE #2:

1. prevent
2. restless
3. Involve
4. Smile, love
5. attention, get it
6. rewards
7. set of rules
8. helper

LEARNING EXERCISE #3:

1. happen
2. students
3. pace
4. Look, gesture
5. hand

6. student's name
7. misbehavior

LEARNING EXERCISE #4:

1. problem
2. interrupts
3. a. Use positive approach.
   b. Ask them to change whatever they are doing.
   c. Change the seating of the student.
   d. Speak in a low, firm voice.
   e. Have them put their heads down.
4. After class
5. Ask for his cooperation.
6. three count
7. a. Don't slap or shhh or yell.
   b. Don't say, "Who did it?"
   c. Don't wait till you have a big problem.
   d. Don't be sarcastic.
   e. Don't threaten or nag.
   f. Don't label children.
   g. Never act exasperated in front of students.
   h. Never grab, shake, spank, slap, jerk, or man-handle a child.

CHAPTER ELEVEN ANSWER KEY

LEARNING EXERCISE #1:

1. set goals
2. deliberate, premeditated, intentional aims that we seek to accomplish
3. beyond, complicated, too simple
4. thought, prayer, awareness, knowledge
5. set a goal
6. complacent, stale, stagnant
7. decisions
8. a. Goals are confidence builders
   b. Goals save time
   c. Goals create a perception so that you are able to see around you the resources that are needed to reach your objectives
   d. Goals provide a sense of order and purpose and motivation over a longer period of time.
   e. Goals with motivation are the wheels that make the world roll.
9. long
10. written down
11. precise
12. measurable
13. published, stated openly, shared

LEARNING EXERCISE #2:

1. accomplish
2. reach, plan
3. a. Make a poster.

b. Pray every day.

c. Set a numerical goal.

d. Set a goal for finding new prospects.

e. Assign prospect responsibility.

f. Phone every prospect.

g. Send mail to every prospect.

h. Visit every prospect.

i. Be enthusiastic.

j. Motivate your students to bring visitors.

k. Have a contest in your class.

l. Determine to pay the price to reach the goal.

4. achievement, satisfaction, blessing

5. Reaching

6. saved, grow

CHAPTER TWELVE ANSWER KEY
LEARNING EXERCISE #1:

1. a. They do not understand the terminology that they hear.

   b. They are frightened into a decision.

   c. They do not understand what sin is; therefore, he really sees no need for a Savior.

   d. They do not realize that they need to make their decision to accept Christ as Savior only once.

   e. They may at the time they go forward, so to speak, feel guilty of one particular sin that they have done.

Answer Key for Learning Exercises   225

      f.   They go for a reward.

      g.   They follow the crowd.

      h.   They want to please someone.

      i.   They had no one teach them after they did accept Christ.

2. lesson

3. close their eyes, bow their heads, raise their hands.

4. clear

5.
   a. Talk with the students individually and ask them why they came forward or raised their hand.
   b. Ask them if they know what sin is and to explain it to you.
   c. Ask them if they have ever sinned.
   d. Tell them we cannot save ourselves by good works.
   e. Explain that we are sinners and need to be saved but can't save ourselves, so Jesus died on the cross to pay for our sins and save us.
   f. Show them that God has given humans a choice to accept Christ or pay the penalty for our sin ourselves in hell.
   g. Ask them if they would like to receive Christ as Savior.
   h. Lead them in the sinners prayer.
   i. Give them some verses for assurance of salvation.

6. terminology, symbolism

7. Ask Jesus to come into your heart.

8. not done

9.   a.   to be taught
       b.   to be visited
       c.   to pray
       d.   to read the Bible
       e.   to live a life pleasing to God
10.   date, verses
11.   Bible
12.   family

CHAPTER THIRTEEN ANSWER KEY
LEARNING EXERCISE #1:

1. improve
2. important
3. retained
4. men, God
5.   a.   student evaluation
       b.   self evaluation
       c.   superintendent evaluation
6. oral participation, written examination
7. thorough, searching, correct, inspiring
8. caution, discretion
9. game
10. minds of many people
11. worst critic
12. best, twice
13. once
14. offence, improvements
15. compliments
16. eager, suggestions, better

ANSWER KEY for CHAPTER REVIEWS

CHAPTER ONE REVIEW:
1. T
2. F
3. F
4. T
5. T
6. F
7. T
8. T
9. T
10. T

CHAPTER TWO REVIEW:
1. F
2. T
3. F
4. T
5. F
6. T
7. T
8. F
9. T
10. T
11. F
12. T
13. T
14. F
15. F
16. T
17. T
18. T
19. T
20. F

CHAPTER THREE REVIEW:
1. T
2. T
3. T
4. F
5. T
6. T
7. T
8. F
14. F
15. T
16. T
17. T
18. F
19. F
20. T
21. T

9. T   22. F
10. T 23. T
11. F 24. T
12. T 25. T or F
13. T

CHAPTER FOUR REVIEW:

1. T   13. T   25. T
2. T   14. T   26. T
3. F   15. F   27. T
4. F   16. T   28. T
5. T   17. T   29. T
6. T   18. T   30. T
7. F   19. T   31. T
8. T   20. F   32. T
9. T   21. T   33. F
10. T 22. T   34. T
11. T 23. F
12. T 24. T

CHAPTER FIVE REVIEW:

1. T   16. T
2. T   17. T
3. T   18. T
4. T   19. T
5. F   20. F
6. T   21. T
7. T   22. T
8. T   23. T
9. T   24. T

10.	T	25.	T
11.	T	26.	F
12.	F	27.	T
13.	T	28.	T
14.	T	29.	F
15.	T	30.	T

CHAPTER SIX REVIEW:

1.	T	13.	T
2.	T	14.	T
3.	T	15.	T
4.	T	16.	T
5.	F	17.	F
6.	T	18.	F
7.	T	19.	T
8.	F	20.	T
9.	T	21.	T
10.	T	22.	T
11.	T	23.	T
12.	T	24.	T
		25.	T

CHAPTER SEVEN REVIEW:

1.	T	14.	T
2.	T	15.	F
3.	T	16.	T
4.	F	17.	T
5.	T	18.	T
6.	T	19.	T
7.	T	20.	T

8. T   21. T
9. F   22. T
10. T 23. T
11. T 24. T
12. T
13. T

CHAPTER EIGHT REVIEW:

1. 2 & 3-year-old
2. 9, 10 & 11-year-old
3. Senior adult
4. Teen
5. 4 & 5-year-old
6. Unmarried
7. 6, 7 & 8-year-old
8. Young Adult
9. Middle Adult
10. Divorced
11. 2 & 3-year-old
12. Senior Adult
13. 9, 10 & 11-year-old
14. Teen
15. 4 & 5-year-old
16. Middle Adult
17. 6, 7 & 8-year-old
18. Young Adult
19. Widowed
20. 2 & 3-year-old
21. 4 & 5-year-old
22. Teens

23. Senior Adult
24. Middle Adults
25 9, 10 & 11-year-old

CHAPTER NINE REVIEW:

1.	T	9.	T
2.	T	10.	T
3.	T	11.	T
4.	F	12.	F
5.	T	13.	T
6.	F	14.	T
7.	T		
8.	T		

CHAPTER TEN REVIEW:

1.	F	13.	T
2.	T	14.	F
3.	T	15.	T
4.	T	16.	F
5.	T	17.	T
6.	T	18.	T
7.	F	19.	T
8.	T	20.	F
9.	T	21.	T
10.	T	22.	T
11.	T	23.	T
12.	T		

CHAPTER ELEVEN REVIEW:

1.	T	13.	T
2.	T	14.	T
3.	T	15.	F
4.	T	16.	T
5.	F	17.	T
6.	F	18.	T
7.	T	19.	T
8.	T	20.	F
9.	T	21.	T
10.	F	22.	T
11.	T	23.	T
12.	T		

CHAPTER TWELVE REVIEW:

1.	F	11.	F
2.	T	12.	T
3.	F	13.	T
4.	T	14.	T
5.	T	15.	F
6.	T	16.	T
7.	T	17.	T
8.	T	18.	T
9.	T	19.	T
10.	T	20.	T

CHAPTER THIRTEEN REVIEW:

1.	F	9.	T
2.	T	10.	T
3.	T	11.	T

4. T   12. T
5. F   13. T
6. T   14. T
7. F   15. T
8. T

FINAL REVIEW ANSWER KEY

1. T	34. T	67. T
2. T	35. F	68. T
3. F	36. F	69. T
4. T	37. T	70. T
5. T	38. T	71. T
6. T	39. T	72. T
7. T	40. T	73. F
8. T	41. T	74. T
9. T	42. T	75. T
10. T	43. T	76. T
11. T	44. T	77. T
12. T	45. T	78. T
13. F	46. T	79. T
14. T	47. T	80. T
15. F	48. T	81. T
16. T	49. T	82. T
17. T	50. T	83. T
18. T	51. T	84. T
19. F	52. T	85. T
20. T	53. T	86. T
21. T	54. T	87. F
22. F	55. T	88. T
23. T	56. T	89. T

24. T	57. T	90. T
25. T	58. T	91. T
26. T	59. F	92. T
27. F	60. T	93. T
28. T	61. T	94. T
29. T	62. .T	95. .T
30. T	63. T	96. T
31. T	64. T	97. T
32. T	65. T	98. F
33. F	66. T	99. T

ABOUT THE AUTHOR...

Dr. Gary R. Jackson is the senior pastor at Liberty Baptist Church of Sarasota, Florida. He founded the church in 1978. He has a PHD and a DMIN. He has been involved in teaching Bible doctrines since 1972.

Exploring the Doctrines ~ Book One
Table of Contents

1. Salvation 7
2. Assurance of Salvation 15
3. Baptism 25
4. Creation 35
5. Prayer 47
6. The Daily Quiet Time 61
7. God's Will 75
8. Backsliding 87
9. Affliction and the Christian 99
10. Temptation 117
11. Lord's Supper 125
12. Grace 135
13. Faith 149

Answer Keys for Study Questions 161

Bibliography 177

About the Author 179

Exploring the Doctrines ~ Book Series

Book Two Lessons	Book Three Lessons	Book Four Lessons
14. Repentance	27. Hell	40. The Rapture
15. Sin	28. Trinity	41. The Bema Seat Judgment
16. Giving	29. God the Father	42. The Marriage of the Lamb
17. Witnessing	30. God the Son (1)	43. The Tribulation (1)
18. The Local Church (1) *History*	31. God the Son (2)	44. The Tribulation (2)
19. The Local Church (2) *Distinctives*	32. God the Holy Spirit (1)	45. The Tribulation (3)
20. The Local Church (3) *Officers*	33. God the Holy Spirit (2)	46. The Battle of Armageddon
21. The Local Church (4) *Growth*	34. The Gift of Tongues	47. The Second Coming
22. The Bible (1) *Inspiration*	35. Bible Memorization	48. The Millennial Kingdom (1)
23. The Bible (2) *King James Version*	36. Sanctification	49. The Millennial Kingdom (2)
24. Man	37. Angels (1)	50. The Great White Throne Judgment
25. Satan	38. Angels (2)	51. The New Heaven and New Earth
26. Heaven	39. The Second Coming of Christ	52. The Dispensational Principle